DOING
BEST
BY
DOING
GOOD

How to Use
Public Purpose
Partnerships
to Boost
Corporate
Profits and
Benefit Your
Community

DOING BEST

BEST

BY

DOING

GOOD

RICHARD STECKEL
and
ROBIN SIMONS

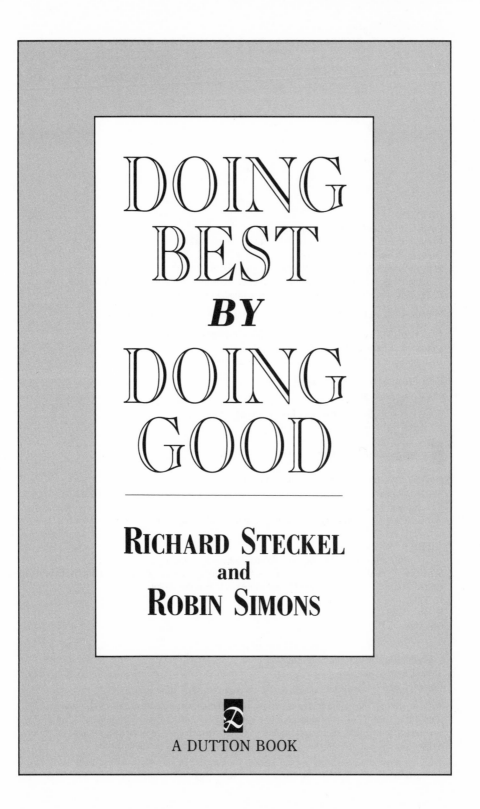

A DUTTON BOOK

DUTTON
Published by the Penguin Group
Penguin Books USA Inc., 375 Hudson Street, New York, New York 10014, U.S.A.
Penguin Books Ltd, 27 Wrights Lane, London W8 5TZ, England
Penguin Books Australia Ltd, Ringwood, Victoria, Australia
Penguin Books Canada Ltd, 10 Alcorn Avenue, Toronto, Ontario, Canada M4V 3B2
Penguin Books (N.Z.) Ltd, 182-190 Wairau Road, Auckland 10, New Zealand

Penguin Books Ltd, Registered Offices: Harmondsworth, Middlesex, England

First published by Dutton, an imprint of New American Library,
a division of Penguin Books USA Inc.
Distributed in Canada by McClelland & Stewart Inc.

First Printing, November, 1992
10 9 8 7 6 5 4 3 2 1

REGISTERED TRADEMARK—MARCA REGISTRADA

LIBRARY OF CONGRESS CATALOGING-IN-PUBLICATION DATA
Steckel, Richard.
  Doing best by doing good: how to use public-purpose partnerships to boost corporate profits
and benefit your community / by Richard Steckel and Robin Simons.
     p.   cm.
  ISBN 0-525-93490-1
  1. Corporations—United States—Charitable contributions. 2. Social responsibility of
business—United States. 3. Social marketing—United States. 4. Corporations, Nonprofit—
United States. 5. Partnership—United States. I. Simons, Robin.
II. Title.
HG4028.C6S716 1992
658.4'08—dc20   92-52877
                                                                                    CIP—

Printed in the United States of America
Set in Century Old Style
Designed by Eve L. Kirch

We dedicate this book to:

Dad and Mom, who provided the right genes and values;

Shelli, Robin, Traci, Jill, Kevin, Taylor, Bob, Hallie, Sylvia, and Thurber, who always offer love and support;

and to the principled business people who make social accountability a natural and important part of their lives.

Contents

Part III. How to Implement a Partnership

Part IV. A Nonprofit Primer

Acknowledgments

We would like to thank the following people who generously gave their time and thoughts in helping us prepare this book: Rhonda Barnat, Tom Barron, Sharon Bialek, Stephen Block, Jan Boylston, Sally Chase, Louise Connor, Susan Corrigan, Mary Elder, Kevin Gavaghan, Susan Gelt, Douglas Horn, Betsy Howland, Jennifer Illidge, John Kazzi, Marjorie Kelly, Lisa Koch, Matt Landon, Robert LeDuc, Jenny Lehman, James Levine, Bob McDaniel, David Miller, Chris Park, Dale Pond, Jonathan Robinson, Bob Rosner, Kathleen Ryan, Dr. Gail Schoettler, Martin Silberman, Esq., Amy Smith, John Statton, Dr. Donald Stevens, and Debbie Williams.

Introduction

For many people, the notion of a partnership between a corporation and a nonprofit organization seems strange. Why would two organizations with such different goals and methods of operation want to work together? What could such a partnership achieve? A quick glance through the advertising inserts that accompany Sunday newspapers gives part of the answer. Most days you'll see one or more ads offering a donation to a nonprofit each time a shopper buys a particular product. "Purchase any bucket of Tyco Super Blocks . . . and we'll donate one dollar to the Child Welfare League of America," proclaims a 1991 ad for Tyco Toys. "Now through Christmas, every time you use the American Express card at Target, American Express will make a five cent contribution to Helping Hugs," promises a 1991 joint promotion by the credit card company and retailer. These companies know that by linking their names, images, and products to causes that consumers care about, they can encourage sales. In a time of stiff corporate competition and unremitting social problems, ties to nonprofit organizations are an effective business building tool.

This type of sales promotion is just one form of public purpose partnership. Licensing agreements, event sponsorships, employee

volunteer programs, and "strategic philanthropy" programs are other
ways companies can align with a nonprofit for mutual benefit. The
range of partnership options is broad, limited only by the partners'
needs and interests. The range of benefits is also broad, from the
marketing gains described above, to the building of employee morale,
to the knowledge that through a public purpose partnership a company
can make a difference in the world.

Over the past fifteen years, we have worked with over a hundred
corporations and nonprofits to develop partnership arrangements. This
book, a distillation of our experience, is designed to help corporate
marketers, philanthropists, human resource managers, and CEOs
learn how partnerships with carefully chosen nonprofits can help a
company contribute to its community while simultaneously strengthening its bottom line.

Pioneering the Partnership Concept

Our foray into public purpose partnerships began in 1977, shortly
after we both arrived at the Denver Children's Museum. The museum, a hands-on learning center for kids, was then three years old
and broke. Knowing this, Richard had just moved his family from California to take the job of executive director.

> I'll never forget my first day on the job. The three grants that made
> up the museum's entire operating budget were about to end. No new
> funds were imminent. The challenge was on: find a way to keep the
> museum afloat.
>
> A quick staff reduction and a couple of small grants from local
> businesses got us through those first few months and bought me
> time to rethink the museum's funding strategy. Clearly, grants—
> government or corporate—were not the way to stability and financial
> health. They were too unpredictable: the museum would always be
> at the whim of outside agencies. Instead, I realized, the museum
> would need to generate its own income. How? By selling products
> and services. In 1976, this was a radical concept for a nonprofit, since

nonprofits traditionally provide services for free or at cost. More radical yet was my notion of who would pay. The market I had in mind was not families, the museum's clientele, but rather corporations—companies that also served families with young children. I believed that the Children's Museum held assets that would be of value to those corporations—its positive, wholesome image and its credibility and expertise in education. I had a hunch that companies that wanted to reach young families would be willing to pay to associate with those intangibles.

My hunch proved correct. Since 1977, the Children's Museum has approached and partnered with close to a hundred corporations, from local family restaurants to Fortune 500 companies. These companies have bought museum exhibits, publications, memberships, and other programs because those products and services helped them market themselves to families. McDonald's, for instance, underwrote museum traveling exhibits, because the exhibits gave the company visibility in schools, places it otherwise could not reach. Local family-oriented businesses bought "storefronts" on "Trick or Treat Street," the museum's safe alternative to trick or treating, because the event helped them reach families in a positive setting. Retailers bought ads in *BOING!,* the museum's national children's newspaper, because it carried their names into homes in a credible educational context. Each of these companies found that Children's Museum products and services helped them reach families in ways their ordinary advertising dollars could not.

Robin joined the museum in 1977 as assistant director.

My job was to oversee the museum's day-to-day operations and to conceive and implement our educational strategies. I quickly discovered that partnerships could be a key component of those strategies: they both funded and disseminated our educational projects. We kept a running list of exhibits, publications, and special programs we felt the museum should develop to fulfill its educational mandate. The million-dollar question was always how to get those projects funded. The answer was another question: *Which companies could benefit by associating with them?*

We constantly scanned the business press for companies that might want the items on our list. For example, we wanted to do a children's activity book that debunked myths about the settling of the American West. Which company would want such a book? How about a local department store that wanted to boost its "back-to-school" business? Indeed, May D&F, a Denver retailer, purchased 10,000 copies and gave them away with every "back-to-school" purchase over $25. By using this Children's Museum product, the store thanked shoppers for using May D&F, encouraged larger purchases, and, most important, reminded families that the company cared about them. From our point of view, the product was equally successful: it provided operating income for the museum and disseminated an important educational message to 10,000 families.

This partnership approach—in which businesses paid for and disseminated Children's Museum products and services because they met corporate marketing goals—quickly became the backbone of museum operations. Partnerships enabled us to produce constantly changing exhibits within the museum, as well as a fleet of traveling exhibits which visited schools, shopping centers, and other children's centers. They enabled us to create a library of educational activity books, which our corporate partners distributed to their customers across the country. And when the museum outgrew its rented home, partnership revenues helped finance the construction of a $3-million, 24,000-square-foot building.

By 1984, the Children's Museum had become a major player on the Denver cultural scene and had developed a national reputation for its "earned income" programs. We were fielding more and more phone calls from people who wanted to learn about the strategy, and were increasingly hired as consultants by groups that wanted to learn how they, too, could develop partnerships with corporations in order to generate revenue and further their missions. To have more time for consulting, we left the museum in 1984 to found AddVenture Network, a for-profit firm specializing in marketing partnerships between corporations and nonprofits. Since then, we have worked with more than 80 clients, including Ben and Jerry's Homemade, a company known as much for its social responsibility as for its ice cream; Chicago's South Shore Bank, a community bank that has won national recognition for its efforts to revitalize inner-city neighborhoods, in part through partnerships with local nonprofit groups; Daybridge Learning Centers, a chain of day-care centers that has developed marketing and educational partnerships with universities, hospitals, and child-development experts; and Stride Rite Corporation, which, in partnership with Wheelock College and Somerville/Cambridge Elder Services, has established the nation's first intergenerational day-care center for employees' children and elderly dependents. Our nonprofit clients have included WNYC, New York City's public radio station, the National Trust for Historic Preservation, the Children's Defense Fund, and the Bishop Museum.

For our corporate clients, partnerships have been an effective adjunct to conventional marketing—a way to reach targeted consumers in the most credible way. They have also bolstered employee morale by inspiring employee pride and giving workers a chance to contribute to a social cause. And they have enabled companies to make a difference in their communities by furthering the work of selected nonprofit organizations. For our nonprofit clients, partnerships have been a powerful vehicle for educating the public about their work, for recruiting members and volunteers, and for generating operating income. Access to corporate resources, including cash, marketing assistance, management skill, and employee volunteers, has multiplied their effectiveness manyfold.

Internal Partnerships

For almost all of our corporate clients, the idea of working with a nonprofit partner was new. These companies had given money to nonprofits; their executives had served on nonprofit boards. But enter a *business relationship with a nonprofit in which both parties benefit equally?* That idea was novel.

Our clients were equally surprised to find that public-purpose campaigns involve a second form of partnership as well—partnerships within the corporation. One of the strengths of public purpose partnerships is that they can meet several corporate needs. In a maximally effective partnership, people from numerous departments—marketing, advertising, public affairs, human resources, corporate giving, government relations, new business development, and perhaps others—sit down together to see where their needs overlap. Then they fashion a partnership that addresses common concerns. Instead of separate departments making separate decisions, departments join their respective strengths and resources in one powerful, multi-purpose program.

A Strategy for the 1990s

Interest in public purpose marketing has surged since Add-Venture's early days. Whereas once our presentations drew crowds of fifteen or twenty, today's audiences often number in the hundreds. The sample materials we bring from past partnership campaigns disappear at an ever faster rate as more people spirit them away to show to colleagues. In just the past three years we have opened offices in Canada, Great Britain, and Australia, in response to calls for our services in each of those countries. Why the growing interest? Because times are tough and partnerships are a powerful tool for tackling both business and social problems.

On the business front, the era of easy money and easy expansion is over. Credit has gotten tighter, consumers are buying less, growth is in short supply. Yet competition is getting tougher: it's tougher to make a better product, to make your product stand out, just to get your message heard. Inside the company, qualified workers are harder to find and retain, and age-old management strategies no longer work. Business as usual has become unusually difficult.

The world outside business has changed just as dramatically. After decades of self-indulgent spending we have recognized that we live in a world of limited resources. Environmental, financial, and health resources are all in short supply. Unfortunately, our inventory of social problems—from homelessness and AIDS to environmental degradation and urban decay—is long and growing. So is consumer demand for solutions. With an activism born in the sixties, consumers are asking business to participate in making the world a better place. They are demanding tuna fish caught without dolphins, products produced without pollution, businesses that embrace their communities and respond to community needs. In many ways, with many voices, they are demanding that business play an active role in solving social problems, because without business participation, solutions may not be possible.

Smart businesses have begun responding. They are creating management systems that give employees greater say in decision-making; giving employees greater flexibility in hours and working styles; adopting child-care and elder-care policies to meet employees' family needs. They are developing "earth-friendly" policies for product sourcing, manufacture, packaging, and waste disposal. They are emphasizing customer service: installing toll-free comment lines, answering complaints with personal letters, instituting no-questions-asked return policies. They are investing in long-term solutions: strengthening public education to create more qualified workers; strengthening inner cities to create healthier communities. They are developing credos of corporate social responsibility, recognizing that they are no longer responsible just to stockholders, but also to stake holders—to the multifaceted communities in which they operate.

And as they become more responsive, they are developing partnerships with nonprofits. Why? Because nonprofits are the new holders of hope in our society. They are the ones on the front lines: they shelter the homeless, nurse the sick, teach the illiterate, nurture the arts. Surrounded by problems, we need their ray of hope.

Nonprofits have suddenly attained a new stature. Individual donations to nonprofits are rising. So is volunteerism. So are employment applications to nonprofit agencies: despite lower salaries and often longer hours, people are leaving the business sector to lend their skills to making the world a better place. A whole new genre of *entrepreneurial* nonprofits has arisen, and they are using traditional business methods to tackle social problems. Target marketing, the establishment of for-profit subsidiaries, the development of licensing agreements, and other strategies borrowed from the business world are the newest weapons in the nonprofit arsenal for battling social ills.

Despite these resources, however, nonprofits can't do their jobs alone. They need the strength of corporations behind them if they're going to make a difference. They need corporate money to help run their programs because traditional funds are drying up. They need corporate volunteers to help them meet the growing needs for service. They need corporate marketers to help them spread the word so they can attract new donors and volunteers. They need influential contacts who can carry their agendas into the halls of government. Nonprofits need the help of business because business, with its money, manpower, talent banks, powerful role in society, is uniquely positioned to help them make a difference. Smart companies are signing up to help—because by helping nonprofits they help themselves.

Getting Started

Companies considering public purpose partnerships have many options. The easiest way to start is by simply adding a partnership element to your philanthropy program—for instance, by choosing grant recipients that strengthen your relationship with target markets. (East River Savings Bank, page 31, uses that approach to build business in a variety of New York neighborhoods.) Companies that want to start with a simple marketing program might try a single, short-term venture designed to bring immediate results. (Procter & Gamble and the Dance Theater of Harlem, page 38, used a short-term campaign to boost product sales for the company and generate desperately needed cash flow for the dance group.) The greatest gains come from long-term, "piggy-back," campaigns in which partners develop a variety of activities over months or even years. (First Constitution Bank's long-term campaign to clean up Long Island Sound, page 40, helped polish the bank's image and attract new accounts.)

You can begin venturing in public purpose partnership at any level. What's important is that you pick your cause and your partner well; that you be clear about your goals; and that you be truthful and sincere with your partner, your public, and yourselves. This book will give you concrete guidelines for beginning a partnership, along with examples and advice from companies that have already gone this way. But keep in mind that we're charting new territory. The very notion of partnerships is in its infancy. Until recently nonprofits lacked the skills and sophistication to make good partners. And corporations didn't need to work for social change. Companies entering public purpose partnerships are the new pioneers. They're mapping the strategies for a new era in business: one in which social responsibility has become a significant factor in a company's bottom line.

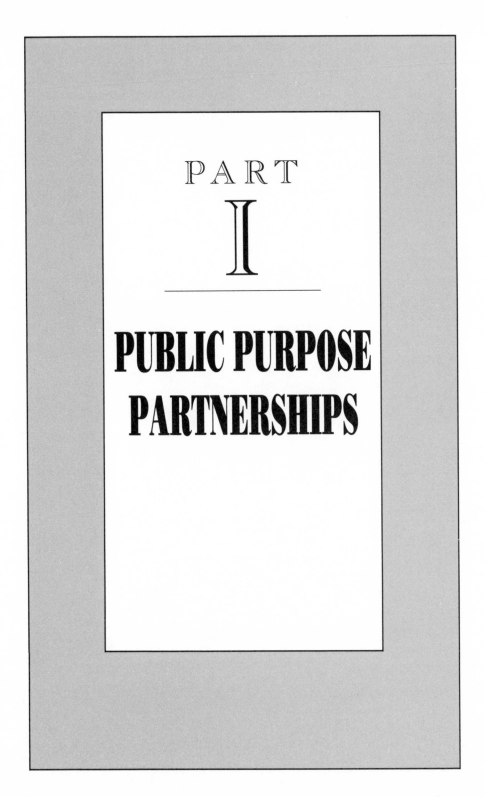

PART

I

PUBLIC PURPOSE
PARTNERSHIPS

CHAPTER 1

Why Establish a Public Purpose Partnership?

(Public purpose partnerships are) a very solid way of making a difference in the community and a good way for Scott to increase its business.

—Nancy Ford, former manager of the Helping
Hand product line, Scott Paper Company

People trust nonprofits. It's almost as simple as that. We tend to believe in what they do, and almost more importantly, in how they do it. They are tackling the most pressing problems of our time for reasons other than personal gain. For this, we tend to grant them respect. We acknowledge their integrity. We give them our trust.

Business, of course, is not so fortunate. We all know that business's bottom line is profit. No matter how altruistic a company may look, when push comes to shove what really counts is money. However, companies that associate closely with nonprofits—that genuinely adopt a nonprofit's cause, that measurably help its work—find that an interesting thing happens. The goodwill accorded the nonprofit rubs off on them. Supporters of the organization begin to look favorably on the company, even to buy its products if that will help the cause. The public at large may see the company in a different light—as one that cares about people as well as about profits. The company's self-centered image is softened; its appeal to consumers grows.

Partnerships also help a company stand out from the crowd. Today, as products become increasingly similar and as ad space becomes increasingly cluttered, partnerships can distinguish a company's products and services from the competition. Since partnerships often get a lot of press, they can give a company a marketing edge.

Partnerships can also help strengthen relationships with employees, who want to feel proud of their employers. Surveys show that companies that are active in their communities are seen as more desirable places to work. With qualified employees getting harder to find and even harder to retain, partnering a nonprofit can give a company a hiring edge.

These are the broad-brush benefits of partnerships. Within each of these categories—image, marketing, human relations—the list of specific benefits is quite long. Partnership campaigns are flexible and can be designed to meet specific corporate needs. What follows is a menu of partnership benefits, and examples of companies that have entered into partnerships with nonprofits to achieve specific goals.

Target Marketing

Every nonprofit has its own following, distinct from that of other organizations. Certainly there are overlaps, but a close examination of the demographics of groups' members will often reveal important differences among them. One benefit of partnering a nonprofit is that it enables you to do targeted marketing.

• Chanel wanted to reach a crowd of wealthy, influential New Yorkers with the launch of a new perfume. Where to go? To the Metropolitan Opera. The design house contributed $250,000 and financed an opening-night fund-raising dinner and fashion show. Both partners profited. The Met received $1.2 million in donations in a matter of hours. Chanel reached exactly the audience it wanted.

• When Revlon wanted to strengthen sales of its Creme of Nature hair products, which are targeted at African Americans, the company offered to make a contribution to the United Negro College Fund (UNCF) for every item sold. Print ads featuring the well-known UNCF slogan, "A mind is a terrible thing to waste," ran in mass circulation as well as black-oriented magazines. In-store displays reinforced the campaign. By linking the products to a cause blacks cared about, the partnership boosted Creme of Nature sales and strengthened Revlon's reputation among African-American consumers.

Enhance Image and Credibility

When corporations rub shoulders with nonprofits, something nice happens: the image of the nonprofit rubs off on the corporation. Corporations can take advantage of this by sidling up to nonprofits that have characteristics they want for their own.

• Compos-it, Inc., is a thirty-person graphic design and typesetting firm in Montgomery, Alabama, which has made partnerships with local arts groups a key component of its business strategy. Each year the company donates $20,000 in in-kind services to local arts organizations. The company's owner, Margaret Carpenter, helped found Jubilee, an annual three-day arts festival. She and other Compos-It employees sit on boards of several arts organizations. "Nobody knew who we were until we became involved with the arts," said Carpenter. "Now we are viewed as *the* quality place in town for graphic design and typesetting work."

Stand Out from the Crowd

In an age of me-too advertising, partnership campaigns can help corporations stand out from the pack. The competition can't duplicate your partnership with a worthy cause. That partnership gives your campaign a personality and a value that can't be matched by conventional ads.

• Few fields are as competitive as the sports shoe industry, where the major manufacturers are in a perpetual race. When inner-city youths began committing crimes to get the money to buy high-priced running shoes, Nike tackled the problem head-on: the corporation formed a partnership with the Boys Clubs of America. In a 1989 campaign called "The Michael Jordan Essay Challenge," Nike donated $1,000 to the Boys Clubs for every point scored by Michael Jordan during an NBA All-Stars game. The money supported programs for inner-city youths. The campaign helped Nike stand out from its competition.

Reinforce Advertising

Once you've introduced a theme in your ads, partnership with a nonprofit can reinforce the theme to consumers.

• In 1988, Reebok introduced the advertising message "We let U.B.U." To reinforce the theme of personal freedom, the corporation developed a partnership with Amnesty International, watchdog for human rights around the world. Reebok spent $10 million to pay off Amnesty International's debts and to sponsor a nineteen-city concert tour featuring some of rock music's biggest stars. Of that $10 million, $2.5 million came from the Reebok Foundation, the rest from marketing budgets. Reebok chose to go low-key on advertising its involvement; it asked only for the line "made possible by the Reebok Foundation" in small type below the tour's title because, as CEO

Joseph LaBonte said, "If we were to do a lot of advertising with our name all over it, it would undo the purity of the event." Nonetheless, the sponsorship—and the tour—received tremendous publicity, creating a strong association between the two groups in consumers' minds.

Increase Consumer Loyalty

By and large, the days of "I'd rather fight than switch" are over. Increasingly critical consumers are being offered a wealth of new products, and it's tougher than ever to keep them loyal to yours. Linking your product to a nonprofit cause can reinforce that loyalty. Besides the general benefits of the association, you can use the nonprofit to create tangible reminders to your buyers of why they're right to do business with you.

• Competition between supermarkets is always tough. While most resort to pricing wars, coupon wars, and other conventional strategies to woo customers, the Denver Division of Safeway Stores developed a more unusual—and longer-term—strategy to build its clientele. The division's campaign focused on families, the bread and butter of the supermarkets' business. Capitalizing on families' loyalty to their schools, in 1990 the division introduced a program called Apples for Students which enables families to earn Apple computers and software for their schools by redeeming Safeway cash register receipts. Each receipt turned in to the school contributes points toward the acquisition of computers. To help schools acquire the computers quickly, Safeway provides monthly student newsletters and suggests ways to get the community involved. The program has helped Safeway build its image as a concerned neighborhood business and has given customers a very tangible incentive to shop at their stores.

Create Cost-Effective Promotions

Many corporations have used self-liquidating premiums to establish a tie with a nonprofit and to recover a portion of their costs. They work with the nonprofit to create a premium item, or purchase a customized premium from the organization. Or they produce a souvenir of a special promotional event, which consumers buy. Sales of the item recover part of the company's outlay, and customers get a lasting reminder of the corporate-nonprofit partnership.

• Looking for a way to promote sales of its Natrel Plus line of deodorants, Gillette (Great Britain) formed a partnership with the World Wildlife Fund (WWF). The company donated £100,000 (approximately $170,000) to the organization and then offered consumers the chance to help as well. Each pack of Natrel Plus deodorant included an offer to buy a WWF T-shirt. From each T-shirt purchase, £1 would be given to the fund. Using this self-liquidating premium, Gillette increased its gift to WWF, established a strong "natural" reputation for the product line, and—not coincidentally—saw sales rise dramatically.

Increase Retail Activity

Partnership campaigns can be used to generate activity at the retail level. For instance, point-of-purchase displays can be developed to advertise the campaign. Discount coupons, event tickets, contest entry forms, or other event items can be picked up or dropped off. Special events can occur in the retail space, and radio and television crews can broadcast from the event. The nonprofit's volunteers can help staff these activities, along with a company's employees, salespeople, retailers, or distributors.

• In 1991 when Procter & Gamble wanted to call attention to the environmental attributes of some of its products, it developed a partnership with Keep America Beautiful (KAB), an environmental group with chapters around the country. First the company announced a cause-related marketing campaign in which money from the sale of selected P&G brands was donated to KAB. To augment the campaign, the company underwrote a national contest in which local KAB chapters and retailers worked together to develop educational programs about the environment. Programs included an "environmental shopping spree" in which four shoppers had three minutes to race through a store and find products whose packaging had the least effect on the environment; a "Run for Recycling," in which teams of shoppers had two minutes to fill grocery carts with items in recyclable containers; and a tree-planting program supplemented with an in-store display of environmental information. The program boosted sales of the featured P&G brands, attracted media attention to participating retailers, and helped strengthen the retailers' image as concerned environmental citizens.

Facilitate Product Launches

Hooking up with a nonprofit can be a particularly effective way to draw consumers' attention to a new product, especially if that product has a specifically targeted market.

• MEM Company, Northvale, New Jersey, manufacturer of cosmetics and perfumes, planned the marketing of a new fragrance even before developing the product. Recognizing the power of environmental concerns, in 1990 MEM concocted a fragrance that would be presented using an environmental theme. Its buyers would be "sensitive, concerned, active and physical men." To promote the new product, Fathom perfume, the company constructed a marketing campaign around sponsorship of a marine conservation center and a tour by an environmental singer and songwriter. MEM bought full-page ads in

GQ and *Outside* magazines, along with a sidebar that invited readers to make pledges to the conservation center's beach cleanup program. Because of the tie-in with the center, MEM also qualified for $250,000 worth of free public service announcements about the project. The results of this strategy? MEM's best product launch since the 1940s.

Facilitate Market Entry

Looking to break into a new market? Tie in with a local nonprofit or cause. Helping a community in an area it cares about can be the fastest way to establish your name and reputation.

• When Continental Airlines reinstated flights from Houston's Hobby Airport, it tied consumer use of the new service to the restoration of the airport's original 1930s art deco terminal. The airline advertised that for every customer who boarded a Continental flight from Hobby during the first seven months of service, Continental would donate from $1 to $5 to the restoration fund. The campaign generated both local and national press for the new service and reinforced the airline's image as a local company that cared about its hometown—an important distinction in a crowded field where even price had ceased to be a differentiator.

Attract Media Coverage

New + worthy = newsworthy. It's corny, but it's true. And that's the magic of public purpose partnership events. They're new and unusual. They benefit a worthy cause. They catch the eye of the media. Partnerships with nonprofits often generate far more coverage than you can get on your own. And, the tie-in with a nonprofit qualifies the event or program for free public service announcements, media placement that would otherwise be prohibitively expensive.

• In 1980 Hallmark Cards, maker of Springbok jigsaw puzzles, in partnership with the Dairy Barn, a small arts center in Athens, Ohio, introduced a line of puzzles featuring designs from award-winning quilts in the Dairy Barn's National Quilt Competition. (A percentage of all sales went to the art center.) To promote the puzzles, managers of the Dairy Barn suggested a National Jigsaw Puzzle Championship, a two-day contest which would draw puzzlers from across the country to compete in the art and sport of puzzling. Both partners hoped that the unusual event would generate press coverage, but neither foresaw just how much. The contest was covered by *The Today Show, Good Morning America, Sports Illustrated,* and newspapers, radio, and TV programs across the country—well beyond what Hallmark could have purchased or received for a conventional promotion.

Reverse Negative Publicity

Some companies have successfully used public purpose partnership campaigns to counteract negative publicity. The local, targeted, and "wholesome" nature of such campaigns makes them especially effective for this use. The one caution: a poorly conceived campaign can backfire, tarnishing the images of the corporation and the nonprofit.

• No sooner had Saddam Hussein invaded Kuwait in August 1990 than gas prices at American pumps jumped—well before American oil companies felt the pinch of the invasion. To quiet the grumbling from consumers, Amoco urged its dealers to support nonprofit causes in their own backyards. Some ten thousand did so by joining Amoco's "Pump-a-Penny" promotion with Children's Miracle Network. For every gallon of gas pumped, the dealers donated a penny to a local children's hospital. While the campaign might not have quelled consumer anger at the price rise, it did soften the blow by contributing to a worthy cause. And it differentiated Amoco from the other gas retailers who had also raised their prices.

Strengthen Community Relations

One way to "localize" a product or service and build community loyalty is to tie it to a community cause.

• K Mart had two goals when it undertook a 1991 partnership with Keep America Beautiful (KAB), the national environmental organization. It wanted to remind consumers about its commitment to sound environmental policies (in 1990 the company had begun a battery recycling program in which it pays consumers $2 for returning used car batteries to the store). It also wanted each store to strengthen its relationship with the local community. As part of the partnership, KAB created a children's recycling kit for K Mart use, containing a coloring book, a hand puppet, a poster, and other educational items. K Mart managers and KAB volunteers took the kit to schools in their communities, where they conducted environmental education programs for students. The program received substantial coverage in local newspapers.

A Way to Entertain Clients

Special events developed in partnership with nonprofits make excellent opportunities for entertaining preferred clients.

• When Boeing Company executives entertain foreign dignitaries, they take their guests to the Museum of Flight, an aviation museum that shares space with the airplane giant on Boeing Field in Seattle. Boeing helped build the museum, which opened in 1987, in part because it offers a lovely place to stroll, take in some airplane history, and slowly get to know a potential business partner. Once a deal is signed, the partners often celebrate with a lavish party in the museum's elegant Great Gallery.

An Opportunity to Mix and Mingle

Nonprofit events also offer corporate executives opportunities to rub shoulders with people they'd like to meet: potential customers, lobbyists, opinion-makers, policy-makers. Gala art and theater openings have long been used for this purpose. As one administrator of a Washington, D.C., cultural institution said, "Let's face it. We're playing matchmaker between corporate lobbyists and government officials." But smaller, more casual events can achieve the same purpose. By strategically picking the nonprofit and the event, you can target the audience you want to reach.

• In 1982 Philip Morris sponsored *The Vatican Collection,* an exhibition at the Art Institute of Chicago that presented several centuries' worth of papal acquisitions. Before the exhibition opened to the public, the company held preview receptions for selected guests, including government officials, religious and business leaders, and other people important to its tobacco and alcohol businesses. The receptions gave Philip Morris a chance to hobnob with these individuals in a positive setting.

• Daybridge Learning Centers is a chain of for-profit day-care centers. To reach prospective families, Daybridge has created a one-day special event, replicable in all its centers, called the Teddy Bear Clinic. The aim of the clinic is to ease children's fears of going to the doctor. The center's partners in each community are local hospitals and universities, which lend pediatricians and child-care experts for the day. The clinic takes place at the local Daybridge center. Families come, toting children and favorite teddy bears. While the parents talk to the experts, the kids help Teddy through his first real doctor's visit. Kids leave with balloons, gifts, and a little more confidence. Parents leave with first-hand experience of the Daybridge center.

Develop New Products

Partnership with a nonprofit can open the doors to new products or product lines.

- F. Schumacher & Co. produces high-quality fabrics, wall coverings, and carpets which are sold through interior designers to residential and commercial customers. In 1984 when Schumacher wanted a new product line, the company went to the National Trust for Historic Preservation. The trust, which owns and manages historic properties, licensed Schumacher to reproduce fabric patterns and artifacts found in its buildings. "Our company benefits because we are able to replicate the fine designs of past artists and we are permitted to create new designs based on traditional elements," said Robert Herring, vice-president of designer relations. The National Trust benefits by receiving operating income from the royalties.

Lower Research and Development Costs

Maintaining in-house research and development departments is extremely costly, affordable by only the biggest companies. However, it is possible to benefit from university research by joining "corporate affiliate" programs at universities. Through these programs, schools make their research available to corporations for an annual fee.

- The granddaddy corporate affiliate program is the one at the Massachusetts Institute of Technology. Several hundred companies pay between $40,000 and $75,000 a year to gain access to MIT research, publications, and professors. Each company is assigned an "industrial liaison officer," who works with the firm to make sure its needs are met. Other universities have similar programs, though not as large or customized.

Improve Employee Retention, Recruitment, and Morale

David Lewin at the UCLA Institute of Industrial Relations studied 188 companies in 1987 and 1989 and found that employee morale was three times higher in companies with a strong degree of community involvement. A 1990 study in Britain conducted by MORI, a British market research firm, found similar results. We shouldn't be surprised. Employees want to feel proud of their employers. In an age so fraught with problems, they want to feel that their companies are forging solutions. Most people also welcome a chance to help. For these reasons, companies are increasingly encouraging employees to volunteer. Employee volunteering is the fastest-growing aspect of corporate-nonprofit partnerships. It stretches the corporate donation, boosts employee morale, and gives much-needed help to the nonprofit cause.

• As a corporate citizen, Apple Computer in Cupertino, California, has long felt a responsibility to its community. In addition to making grants of money and equipment to nonprofit organizations, Apple strongly encourages employees to volunteer. The Employee Volunteer Action program is run out of the community affairs office. Each month Apple employees receive a newsletter that describes local volunteer opportunities. Employees who volunteer consistently for an organization for six months or longer may request a grant of up to $500 for that organization.

• Dow Chemical Company encourages its employees to volunteer in a program even closer to home. In partnership with the Wildlife Habitat Enhancement Council (WHEC), Dow is preserving and restoring wildlife habitats on corporate property. The company owns 860 acres near Joliet, Illinois, which contains wetlands, woodlands, and grasslands. With the help of WHEC, Dow employees are building nesting boxes, conducting controlled burns, and providing other needed labor to restore the property to habitat condition.

- The Polaroid Corporation has taken a different approach to employee involvement. Each year the company foundation gives approximately $2 million to community, educational, and cultural organizations near its home in Boston. Decisions about who gets the grants are made by a grant review committee composed of Polaroid employees.

Create Employee Perks

Partnership campaigns also provide opportunities to reward employees with perks. Free or discounted tickets, special admissions, private classes, exclusive parties, chances to meet celebrities, and other benefits are usually easy to design into partnership promotions. All of these boost employees' loyalty and reward them for their service.

- Bell Cellular of Canada uses employee volunteers when it sponsors special events, such as symphony concerts and art exhibitions. The volunteers run hospitality tables, talk with guests, and hand out discount coupons and literature about Bell's products. Volunteers are required to commit 100 hours of their own time and are trained by Bell staff in both sales and hospitality skills. As compensation they get admission to the events, souvenirs, and recognition in performance reviews. The volunteer positions are so popular that Bell has three times more applicants than it can use. The volunteers have also provided some unexpected benefits to the company. They have saved Bell the $100,000 (Canadian) that it would have paid to hire outside staffers; and because they are knowledgeable about the company, they have produced $1 million (Canadian) in additional sales.

Of course, corporations are not the only ones to profit from these partnerships. Partnership campaigns provide substantial benefits to their nonprofit partners as well.

Increased Operating Income

The biggest benefit of partnerships to nonprofits is money. Few nonprofits will lend their names and reputations to a corporation without getting a substantial monetary return. What makes the money particularly valuable is that it is unrestricted. Unlike grants and contract funds, which must be applied to particular programs, money from a campaign can be used for whatever the organization desires. As a rule, it's used for general operations, the hardest thing to fund.

Increased Visibility

Partnership campaigns draw attention to the nonprofit. Many people hear about the organization for the first time and subsequently become members, donors, or volunteers. For example, Philadelphia-based Big Brothers Big Sisters of America reported that inquiries to the organization rose 30 percent in 1987 after a cause-related marketing campaign with Arby's, the fast-food chain.

Public Education

Partnership campaigns can help nonprofits disseminate their educational messages to much wider audiences than they would reach on their own. If thousands of people hear about the organization through its regular communications—primarily mailings and newsletters—millions can hear and read about it through a partnership campaign. Print ads, television commercials, point-of-purchase displays—all cast a wide net.

Diversified Income Base

Most nonprofits have relatively few sources of income. They depend for the bulk of their revenue on grants and donations. Since both of these sources are unpredictable (and shrinking), the organizations are financially vulnerable. Adding a third—earned—source of income strengthens their financial health.

Experience in Managing Promotional Campaigns

In mounting a campaign, the for-profit and nonprofit partners work closely. The nonprofit lends image, credibility, and legwork; the for-profit brings money, resources, and expertise at managing massive promotional campaigns. Through their involvement, nonprofit managers learn valuable promotional skills that can help them get their message heard—by the public, by donors, by policy-makers—in the future.

Attractiveness to Future Donors and Business Partners

A successful campaign makes a nonprofit more attractive to future partners, whether those partners are donors, contractors, or corporations. Funders want to know that the organizations to which they give money are fiscally sound, with proven track records for raising, earning, and managing money. Success in a partnership campaign says that the nonprofit has diversified its income base and is less reliant on donors' help. The San Jose Symphony, for example, raised an unexpected $107,000 in donations after a 1981 American Express cause-related marketing campaign.

Advertisement reprinted with permission of the United Negro College Fund.

Reinforcement of Business Skills

As nonprofits become more businesslike in their operations, partnership with corporations helps reinforce new skills. Decision-making processes are streamlined. Management systems are refined. Short- and long-term planning processes are upgraded. Overall financial sophistication grows.

CHAPTER 2

Three Case Studies

East River Savings Bank: Making Philanthropy More Strategic

East River Savings Bank has always thought of itself as a neighborhood bank. Founded in New York City in 1848, the bank has long subscribed to the belief that "our business is helping people." In this case, that means a wide diversity of people. The bank's sixteen branches in the New York metropolitan area operate in neighborhoods as diverse as they come, from Little Italy in lower Manhattan, to a largely Asian neighborhood in Queens, to Manhattan's tony Upper East Side.

Besides providing banking services to this patchwork quilt of neighborhoods, East River has a long history of community philanthropy, giving many small grants annually to local causes. With a small corporate giving budget—and a large number of requests—the bank was always in the uncomfortable position of having to choose among many worthwhile requests. To alleviate this problem, the bank decided to redesign its program. Rather than give money reactively to a hodgepodge of causes, East River decided to become more proactive in its giving. The managers believed that if the bank learned more about its neighbors and their needs—and then designed programs in response—it would achieve two things. It would better help the groups who asked for support, and it would better help itself by building stronger relationships with new and existing depositors. To implement the new program, East River installed Rhonda Barnat as manager of community affairs and gave her the following mandate: strengthen our corporate giving program so that it garners favorable press, attracts positive public opinion, and benefits the diverse communities in which we do business.

Strategic Philanthropy in Action

To give the new program greater impact, the bank decided to focus all its grants in one area. What should that area be? Barnat surveyed the bank's neighborhoods. One thing stood out almost immediately: almost every neighborhood on the bank's map had been shaped by immigrants. Whether it was a community of recent immigrants like the Korean neighborhood near the Queens branch, or a much older community like Little Italy, to which residents had come a hundred years before, every neighborhood was colored by the immigrant experience. And although the neighborhoods were distinctly different from each other, one feature stood out as common to them all: the importance of education. Each neighborhood had used education as a springboard to success in America. The bank decided to honor that commitment to education by focusing all its giving there— on educational projects that met the specific needs of individual neighborhoods.

HIGH-SCHOOL SCHOLARSHIPS

East River's first project was a fairly traditional one for a savings bank: a high-school scholarship program. The bank approached high schools in several neighborhoods and asked them to select students to receive college scholarships. To reinforce the bank's business interest, it offered the scholarships in the form of savings accounts. The program was fairly simple, but the results were impressive. The scholarships generated much goodwill by making it possible for neighborhood sons and daughters to go to college. They also generated a tangible return for the bank: new savings accounts, new depositor relationships with the students' families, and considerable positive press in neighborhood newspapers. Most important, the program gave each branch (and each branch manager) a lot of very positive visibility right in its own backyard.

THE ACADEMIC EXCELLENCE PROGRAM

Buoyed by the success of the high-school scholarships, East River decided to gear the program up a degree. The bank approached the City University of New York (CUNY) with the idea of recognizing people who were graduating from the university's GED (high-school equivalency) program and giving them scholarships to use in college. The bank developed this idea for several reasons. One was that the program epitomized the bank's focus on neighborhood-relevant education: many of the GED graduates were immigrants from East River's neighborhoods. Scholarships would make a big difference to those GED graduates, and would also engender more goodwill in the neighborhoods. Another benefit of the program was that it gave the bank an opportunity to develop a relationship with CUNY, a leading institution in New York.

So with CUNY, the bank developed the East River Savings Bank Academic Excellence for GED Students Scholarship Program, which offers ten $1,000 scholarships to students selected by the GED program from among the 2,000 who graduate each year. Although $1,000 doesn't sound like a lot of money toward college tuition, at CUNY it goes a long way. As with the high-school grants, the scholarships are offered in the form of savings accounts, and the bank supplements each one with the offer of a student loan. In its third year, as of this writing, the program has rewarded the bank with a stable pool of deposit and loan relationships.

The program also captures a great deal of positive press. Because the students' stories tend to be uplifting and heartwarming, the program has high news value both citywide and in each student's neighborhood. The program has also given East River a positive continuing relationship with CUNY.

BEST-SELLING AUTHORS

East River's next project was of a very different nature—to suit a very different type of neighborhood. In 1991 community affairs manager Rhonda Barnat wanted a project that would solidify the bank's relationship with Manhattan's Upper East Side, a neighborhood of well-to-do, well-educated professionals. What kind of project would appeal to them? As Barnat examined the neighborhood's needs, interests, and resources, she focused on Marymount College, a small private college in the heart of the community. The bank knew Dr. Regina Peruggi, president of the college, from its work with CUNY, and also knew that Marymount's auditorium was frequently the site of public programs. Could the bank sponsor a program at the auditorium that would serve the neighborhood, serve the college, *and* strengthen the bank's relationship with local depositors? You bet it could. With the college, the bank developed the Marymount Writers' Series, a series of free lectures by best-selling authors, such as Dominick Dunne (popular chronicler of life on the Upper East Side), Cynthia Ozick, Gay Talese, and Erica Jong. Writers were selected because they were local and appealed to the urban tastes of neighborhood residents. Although the budget for the program was small—$10,000, including $2,000 in in-kind donations—its impact was impressive. In a city where big bucks can buy you a lecture almost every night of the week, free lectures by best-selling authors are seen as a genuine community service.

The series brought genuine returns to the bank as well. It cemented the bank's relationship with its affluent neighbors: numerous thank-you letters told Barnat she had made a smart move. And it created a business relationship with Marymount College, a well-endowed institution with a variety of banking needs. In fact, the success of the Writers' Series led the bank to create a second lecture series that year, on scientific and technical literacy. This one was held at Iona College in New Rochelle, where the bank has its corporate headquarters. With help from Dr. Victor Stanionis, then chair of Iona's physics department, the series presented such sought-after speakers as Benoit Mandelbrot, the well-known originator of chaos theory. Again, by targeting the series to the interests of the neighborhood, and by using its small budget strategically, the bank parlayed a $10,000 donation into a public relations coup.

THE GRANT FOR ENGLISH AS A SECOND LANGUAGE

A fourth community led to the creation of yet a different type of program. This time East River was searching for a way to help its neighborhood in Queens, a community heavily populated by Korean immigrants. By putting out feelers to the community, Rhonda Barnat found the Korean YWCA, a hub of neighborhood activity. As she talked to Y leaders, it became clear that one of the biggest needs in the neighborhood was for instruction in the English language. So the bank gave the Y an $8,000 grant to offer classes in English as a second language (ESL). The money could not have been better spent. Not only did the classes fill to capacity with delighted students, but the amount of good publicity generated by the grant was unexpectedly large. By working with a trusted organization in the community and funding a program that was very much in demand, the bank cracked the culture barrier that normally keeps "establishment" institutions outside ethnic neighborhoods. Once inside, community networking and communication channels gave the bank tremendous recognition. All five neighborhood newspapers picked up the story of the donation; a neighborhood slide show praised it, and it was covered on local cable TV.

East River further pleased residents with offers of student loans to ESL graduates. At the bank's invitation, Edward C. Sullivan, chairperson of the Higher Education Committee of the New York State Assembly, spoke to the Y about higher education and the advantages of loans. To residents, this was further proof of the bank's commitment to their needs. For the bank, of course, it was a solid business opportunity.

The Process

Rhonda Barnat, whose job has grown to include marketing as well as community affairs, and her staff of three (an assistant, a secretary, and a graphic designer) manage approximately forty projects a year. Some are more labor-intensive than others. The group's job is to conceive the projects, find the partners, and oversee implementation. "The stakes are very high, working with community groups," said Barnat. "There are a lot of things that can go wrong"—especially since the bank relies on the groups to implement the projects and each project reflects the bank's image. Barnat added, "In this program, we have no room for failures." To minimize problems, she and her staff have developed a number of strategies which, they believe, contribute to the program's success.

1. *They seek opportunities.* Rather than waiting for community groups to approach them, the bank constantly scans its neighborhoods, looking for projects and partners. As Barnat said, "We cook up these projects at the bank; we don't wait for people to come to us."

2. *They pick their partners carefully.* Picking the right partners is crucial to the bank's success. The bank is looking for partners, not just grantees, so Barnat's group looks for the following qualities:

- The partners must be respected in their neighborhoods: the bank is tying its image and programs to these organizations, so the organizations must be first-class.
- The partners must be sensitive to the bank's needs: they must understand that the bank needs to review all program elements for appropriateness, and adherence to bank standards. (On the few occasions when this has been a problem the bank has ended the partnership.)
- The partners must have "staff capacity": the bank relies on the neighborhood groups to carry out the events, so the groups must have enough people to do the required work. This doesn't mean they have to be large. The bank realizes that many nonprofits are small and understaffed, so it looks for a high level of staff commitment to the organization and the project, "peo-

ple who will come in on a holiday if that's what a project needs."

3. *They evaluate prospective partners quickly.* The bank approaches a prospective partner with an idea for a project and then works with the partner to refine it. If during this process Barnat's group suspects that the relationship will be difficult, it ends the relationship immediately. "We can harm the group—and the bank—by continuing a bad relationship," Barnat said. Signs of a bad relationship? Inflexibility and insensitivity to the bank's needs. Sign of a good relationship? "We like them! We feel like we want to work with them and feel we can work with them well."

4. *They promote each campaign heavily.* The bank works closely with its partners to promote the campaigns. Barnat's group asks each partner to write press releases. These must be submitted to the bank for review and are often rewritten by bank personnel. They are then released by the community organization on its own stationery to neighborhood and city news media and to other special-interest outlets. The bank also buys advertising for the campaigns in neighborhood papers. Because of the novelty of the programs, the bank often finds itself featured on the evening news. "We're the only GED scholarship program in the country," Barnat noted. "It's a great news story. We couldn't buy that kind of advertising."

The Future of Strategic Philanthropy

Will East River Savings Bank continue its strategic philanthropy? Absolutely. The program will never completely replace "pure" philanthropy: the bank will always fund pet projects with no expectation of return. But East River's managers see themselves moving more and more in the direction of linking marketing and philanthropic concerns. Why? The program provides more than money to the nonprofit partners, and more than positive exposure for the bank. "This is not a wonderful time for banks—or for any type of business," Barnat pointed out. "And as dollars get scarcer, every dollar has to work harder."

Procter & Gamble: Entering a Short-Term Partnership with Dance Theater of Harlem

The winter of 1990 was a tough time for Dance Theater of Harlem (DTH). The dancers in this highly acclaimed black dance company were used to cash shortages. Threats of layoffs and curtailed seasons were standard fare. But the winter of 1990 was worse than others, and before DTH's first performance of the season, company founder Arthur Mitchell announced that due to lack of operating funds, he was canceling the entire season. The dance world, particularly in the company's home territory of New York and northern New Jersey, was dumbfounded. Rallying cries went out to help the company get back on its feet.

Enter Procter & Gamble. The giant consumer products company was looking for a way to bolster sales of Tide with Bleach, particularly in the Northeast, and particularly among African Americans. In the dance company's plight Burrell Advertising, a division of Burrell Communications Group, P&G's advertising agency, saw an opportunity. Burrell believed that with a strategically designed partnership, Procter & Gamble could help itself and the dance company at the same time.

The partnership would take the form of a short-term multifaceted marketing campaign linking Dance Theater of Harlem with Tide with Bleach. The campaign would be developed and implemented, turnkey fashion, by Burrell. It would be paid for with marketing dollars from the Tide brand group. The dance company agreed.

A Multifaceted Marketing Campaign

The centerpiece of the campaign would be an in-store sales promotion, which would run for six weeks in 500 stores in African-American neighborhoods in New York and northern New Jersey. This decision was made for several reasons. P&G believed that this would be the best way to reach the targeted African-American community. As one person at Burrell said, "People may not read the newspaper.

They may not watch TV. But everybody's got to eat. Everybody goes to the grocery store." An in-store campaign would also have the greatest impact on sales. It would provide an easy way to encourage consumers to make individual donations to DTH. And it would involve retailers, a critical link in P&G's distribution system.

Vital to the in-store campaign were brochures distributed to each participating store. The brochures talked about the financial straits of Dance Theater of Harlem and told consumers they could help the dance company in two ways. One was by making an individual contribution, using the form included in the brochure; P&G would match these individual donations. The second was by purchasing Tide with Bleach, using the coupon in the brochure. The company promised to give $.35 to DTH for every coupon redeemed, up to a ceiling of $50,000. The brochure was supplemented by "shelf talkers," cards that dangled from shelves where Tide with Bleach was sold, describing the sales promotion program.

P&G supplemented the in-store campaign with a TV commercial featuring a performance by DTH dancers. One of the dancers then used Tide with Bleach to get the ground-in dirt out of her dancing socks—compelling evidence of what Tide could presumably do for an average person's dirty clothes.

The company also bolstered the campaign with public service announcements. These free media placements, which are available to nonprofit organizations, were prohibited from advertising Procter & Gamble's product or its sales promotion efforts; instead, they focused on the dance company. By raising public awareness of DTH's problems, P&G strengthened the community appeal of its sales promotion campaign.

DTH had already decided to publish a coffee-table book filled with photographs of the dancers; sales of the book would benefit the company. P&G underwrote the costs of publishing the book, as well as the costs of a September 1990 fund-raising reception at which the book would be introduced. Introduced as well was the P&G-DTH partnership. At the star-studded event, which was attended by Joyce Dinkins (wife of New York mayor David Dinkins), Gregory Hines, Melba Moore, and other African-American luminaries, the company announced the sales promotion campaign and showed the DTH commercial.

When the campaign was over, donations to DTH triggered by sales of Tide with Bleach had reached the $50,000 ceiling. Individual contributions were small—just under $5,000. The partnership had produced a variety of income streams for the dance company: the cause-related marketing donation, the individual donations, the fee for performing in the commercial, and the revenue from sales of the book. Just as important, it had broadcast the dance company's difficulties, and many people had responded. As a result of the campaign, the number of individual supporters of the dance company grew substantially.

P&G was equally happy. The campaign had not only had a positive effect on sales of Tide with Bleach, but had also created goodwill in the company's target market. The strategists at Burrell believe that by providing a benefit to the community, the campaign created a strong bond between African Americans and the Tide brand. They consider the partnership a highly effective target marketing tool and an equally effective way of providing much-needed support to Dance Theater of Harlem.

First Constitution Bank: Developing a Continuing Partnership with Long Island Sound

Had you told the employees of New Haven's First Constitution Bank in 1988 that they would soon be responsible for the formation of a U.S. Environmental Protection Agency office dedicated to Long Island Sound, they would have called you crazy. But over the next three years, Long Island Sound became a key part of the bank's marketing strategy. The success of the program—for the sound, the bank, and several nonprofit partners—brought waves of acclaim for all involved.

Linking Business with the Cause

The program got its start in 1988 when the bank was approached by the Mystic Marine Aquarium in Mystic, Connecticut, to help it fund a whale study center. Interested in whales, and sensing a marketing opportunity, the bank's new CEO, Walter Miller, agreed. But rather than just write out a check, Miller decided to get the community involved. Whales, after all, were Connecticut's state mammal. People rarely resisted a chance to help them. Suppose the bank linked its donation to the opening of new accounts? It would give the public a chance to help, give the bank a popular cause with which to associate—*and* build business.

So, in partnership with the aquarium, the bank launched Operation Whale Save, a two-part cause-related marketing campaign to raise money for the new whale study center. The bank advertised that each time someone opened a qualifying account, the depositor would get a free toy whale and the bank would donate money to the center. The same would happen when someone applied to the bank for a loan. At the same time, all twenty-five bank branches were equipped with a television and a VCR so that they could show a program developed by the bank about the aquarium narrated by TV star William Conrad.

The campaign was extremely successful. Besides boosting business for the bank and raising funds for the aquarium, Operation Whale Save generated tremendous public recognition. Newspaper reporters, writers in environmental journals, and public officials acclaimed the partnership for its efforts to save the whales and involve the public in environmental action. Buoyed by this success, First Constitution decided to expand its environmental marketing efforts the following year.

CAUSE-RELATED MARKETING PLUS

In 1989 First Constitution launched a program called Help Save Our Sound (HSOS). The "social" goal of HSOS was to generate public awareness of and support for the restoration and preservation of Long Island Sound, one of Connecticut's most valuable—but polluted—resources. The program's marketing goal was to strengthen the bank's image and business in its home state. Its nonprofit partners were the Nature Conservancy and the Long Island Soundkeepers Fund, two reputable environmental groups working to protect the sound.

Help Save Our Sound was structured much like Operation Whale Save. With a cause-related marketing campaign at its core, the program made donations to the two organizations each time someone opened a new account or applied for a loan. But then the program branched out.

ADDING A PREMIUM

As an added inducement—and an added educational opportunity—the bank gave a Recycling Handbook to each new depositor. The twenty-page booklet opened with a letter from the bank's CEO explaining the bank's commitment to Long Island Sound and the HSOS program, then offered tips on how to conserve, reuse, and recycle household items.

SPONSORED ADVERTISING

The Recycling Handbook was produced for the bank by the Connecticut Fund for the Environment. The last page bore a full-page ad for the organization, describing its work and soliciting memberships.

A bank mailer and lobby brochure described the HSOS campaign and gave tips for saving water. It also included full-page descriptions of the Nature Conservancy and the Long Island Soundkeepers Fund and a mail-in form for making donations or becoming a volunteer for the two organizations.

The effect of these sponsored ads was not only to raise awareness and donations for the organizations, but also to reinforce the bank's commitment to the cause and strengthen its image as a good public citizen.

SPECIAL EVENTS

The bank used special events to expand the campaign's reach, sponsoring numerous beach cleanups during the summer of 1989, as well as a children's art contest. These events drew people the bank might otherwise not have reached and attracted media coverage. They also provided numerous opportunities for the bank to reinforce its association with the cause.

The bank also used a special event to reach another important audience: legislators. In late 1989 it held the first State of the Sound Address, a public event, well covered by the media, that provided a forum in which state and national lawmakers could talk about their actions to protect the environment.

Through the event, the bank positioned itself as a business leader on the environment. It announced its own in-house recycling program and its decision to stop using Styrofoam, balloons, and other nonrecyclable products that could harm Long Island Sound. The bank also challenged businesses across the state to examine the impact of their own operations on the environment and to begin recycling efforts and other environmental programs of their own. Essentially, the bank used the event to position itself as part of the solution to environmental problems, rather than part of the problem.

HELP SAVE OUR SOUND: YEAR II

First Constitution launched the second year of HSOS at New Haven's Earth Day 20 concert, in April 1990, a fund-raiser and public education event that the bank sponsored. In advertisements for the concert, the bank announced the continuation of the cause-related campaign to benefit its two environmental partners. As before, new depositors and loan customers spurred donations to the nonprofits and received the Recycling Handbook.

Also as before, the bank boosted its marketing and social responsibility efforts with a special event. This time it was the statewide Hands Around the Sound, cosponsored with local media to raise money for and educate the public about cleaning up the sound. The event included beach cleanups all along the Connecticut coast, formation of a human chain along the shoreline to call attention to the problem, and a petition drive to create a government office to oversee the cleanup of the sound. Later that fall, a formal ceremony presenting the petitions to the state legislature was conducted at the bank—one more opportunity for media coverage, reinforcing First Constitution's good-guy image.

MAKING WAVES

The results of the Help Save Our Sound campaign were extremely positive. A 1990 survey of First Constitution's customers indicated that a majority of new accounts had been opened because of the HSOS program, and that the bank's name and image were strongly and positively associated with the environmental program.

The cause-related marketing campaigns raised $50,000 for the Nature Conservancy and the Soundkeepers Fund. Additional money came from other, independent fund-raising events prompted by HSOS. Teenagers, local environmental groups, and other companies in New Haven called the bank to ask whether they could hold their own fund-raisers and give the money to HSOS. Several bank customers also wrote the cause into their wills—possibly the first unsolicited bequests in bank history!

Then, of course, there is the EPA office. As a result of First Constitution's petition drive, the U.S. Environmental Protection Agency announced that it would open a New Haven office to oversee the cleanup of Long Island Sound. More publicity. More acclaim. More evidence that First Constitution was right to pursue this long-term multilayered public purpose partnership.

CHAPTER 3

Why Establish a Public Purpose Partnership Now?

In the eighties everybody still felt they had a chance to get rich themselves. Now, with the economy in the state it's in, the stock market in the doldrums, land values falling, white-collar layoffs and so on, people are starting to recognize that the train has pulled out of the station—and they weren't on it.

—David Meer, senior vice-president, DYG, Inc., a consumer
research and consulting firm in Elmsford, New York

This is the decency decade. Buyers demand to know where a company stands before they purchase its products.

—Lesa Ukman, president, International Events Group,
publisher, Special Events Report

The 1980s were the businessperson's dream decade: a time of rapid growth, climbing stock prices, and market expansion. The eighties were the decade when a new mail-order catalog came out every week; when a new industry developed every month; when a new entrepreneur smiled from the cover of business magazines almost every issue.

It was a time when it was easy to find customers. Some seventy-six million baby boomers, raised on Saturday-morning commercials, suddenly had cash in their pockets: *they wanted to buy!* It was easy to find good employees: baby boomers flooded the workforce: many were eager to work hard, eager to get ahead. And it was easy to be selfish. With so many people who were young, single, and self-absorbed, why not be? Problems like poverty and illiteracy seemed far away in a country that had grown used to postwar affluence.

It was a decade in which every market force, every cultural trend, even every governmental initiative, conspired to bolster business profits. Who couldn't prosper in times like that?

But like all good things, it had to end. The decade that began with unprecedented business proliferation ended with massive mergers, acquisitions, and bankruptcies. Millions of people lost their jobs. New jobs were harder to find; new salaries were lower. Affluence, once seemingly so close, became elusive. The 1990s rolled in, bearing cultural and economic changes that will reshape business for the rest of the decade. Let's look at those changes, and the challenges they present for American corporations.

Challenge #1: The Growth Slowdown

Is it harder to do business in the nineties? You bet it is. Four forces are slowing the wheels of production.

1. The population slowdown. The baby boomers, seventy-six million strong, were followed by a much smaller generation, the baby-busters. Today there are millions fewer people entering the work force, millions fewer people establishing households and buying products. The market is shrinking.

2. The cash shortage in state and local governments. During the seventies and eighties, local governments created programs that promoted business: they incubated entrepreneurs, offered tax breaks to attract companies, and deregulated business. These days, few governments can afford such largesse. Most are struggling to balance their budgets and using whatever cash they have to fight the rising tide of economic, social, and infrastructure problems threatening to drown their communities. Don't look to government for help now.

3. The federal deficit. In the past, when all else failed and the economy was in the doldrums, the federal government *bought* back its health through deficit spending. But with the federal deficit estimated at $399 billion in 1992, that approach is now unworkable.

4. The tightness of credit. Having taken a beating on bad loans, banks (and their regulators) have made it tougher to borrow money. Even established businesses with proven track records are having difficulty getting loans. This tightening of business credit constricts the flow of capital from private investors. The result: less money for expansion, creating a cycle of slower growth.

But is slow growth no growth? Not necessarily. Astute business-people will find avenues for expansion despite the tough times. They will do so by deepening relationships with customers; by emphasizing service, quality, and convenience; and by strengthening the intangible assets that set them apart from the competition. One of the tools will be nonprofit partnerships.

Challenge #2: The Climate of Caring

If the eighties were the decade of greed and selfishness, the nineties are the decade of caring and sharing. The signs are all around us: volunteerism is up sharply; so is charitable giving. Socially responsible investment funds are attracting record capital. Consumers are spending more money to buy products that protect the environment. If people pined for a BMW before, they now yearn for a simpler lifestyle with less emphasis on material success.

Fueling this trend is anger about the *unfairness* of the eighties. While millions of people lost their jobs to corporate mergers, their houses to recessionary markets, and their savings to bank closings, other people became millionaires at their expense. In defiance, people have adopted antimaterialist values in which the things that matter most are things that money can't buy. According to a 1989 opinion poll by Research & Forecasts for Chivas Regal, a Seagram Brand, 62 percent of working Americans now believe that the most important indicator of success is not a job title, not a car, not the right address, but a happy family life.

The trend is also fed by a growing list of seemingly insurmountable social ills. The number of poor Americans grew by 2 million during the 1980s; housing costs have doubled or tripled in most metropolitan areas, forcing millions of Americans onto the streets; AIDS is claiming more than 25,000 lives a year at a time when 37 million Americans lack health insurance; the U.S. infant mortality rate is among the highest in the developed world; 73 million Americans are either marginally or functionally illiterate; in some of our biggest cities—Boston, Chicago, Detroit and New York—high school dropout rates range between 40 and 60 percent; nearly 3,800 teenagers drop out of American high schools each day.

We see it in consumer surveys: according to a 1990 Roper poll, 52 percent of U.S. consumers would pay 10 percent more for a socially responsible product; 67 percent are concerned about a company's social performance when they shop. A 1990 survey by Century Research of 600 New Yorkers found that 25 percent had stopped buying the products of at least one company because they believed the company wasn't a good environmental citizen.

We see it in the resounding success of *Shopping for a Better World*, the book first published in 1989 by the nonprofit Council on Economic Priorities that rates 1,300 companies according to social criteria (including charitable giving, advancement of women and minorities, military contracts, environmental policies, and animal testing). According to research conducted by the Council, nearly seventy percent of the book's readers report changing their buying habits based on the book's ratings.

We see it in the success of consumer boycotts—against tuna companies that fail to screen their catch for dolphins, against companies that manufacture products with chlorofluorocarbons, against companies that fail to clean up toxic waste.

THE MAIN DETERRENTS, 1990

Base: 1,336 adults

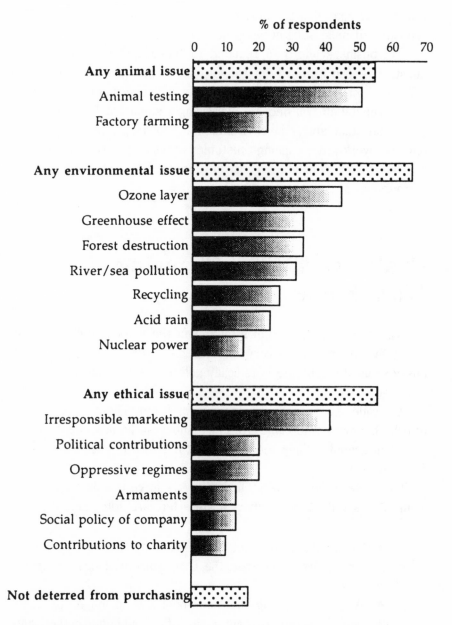

% of respondents

Source: BMRB/Mintel

"The Green Consumer 1991," Mintel International Group

We have seen the rise of the caring consumer who uses his or her wallet to demand that business change. It must not only stop creating problems. It must start creating solutions.

Can business afford to respond to these demands? The better question is, can it afford not to? Growth in the nineties and beyond will come from strengthened relationships with consumers, and a company's reputation will become increasingly important to its success. Companies that invest in environmental controls, community development, work-force training, customer service, and responsible citizenship will buy consumer loyalty in years to come. They'll find public partnerships a useful way to do that.

Challenge #3: The Changing Work Force

Want to talk change? Let's talk about the work force, an area in which every "given," every expectation, every formula by which business used to operate is radically different from what it was a decade ago.

A decade ago, workers were a dime a dozen. There were millions of baby boomers who came from nice suburban homes, went to nice suburban schools. They took a job and did it, few questions asked, few demands made.

Those were the old days. Today's work force is a different story. Tomorrow's will be more different still. Here are some statistics:

- Today the labor pool is *shrinking* by 500,000 workers a year. For the first time ever, the U.S. economy faces a shortage of workers.
- Workers entering the labor pool are no longer predominantly white males; 90 percent of work-force additions in the 1990s will be women and members of minorities. Many of the minority members will be immigrants.

- One out of three Americans is functionally or "marginally" illiterate—lacking basic skills for employment.
- Over the next decade, millions of workers will retire and will be replaced by less skilled younger workers.

What does this mean for business? As these new workers join the labor pool, they bring a whole new set of needs, previously unfelt in corporations:

- With the increasing numbers of working women, employees demand increasing attention to the needs of the family: already companies are offering child care, elder care, flexible time, and flexible benefits for helping employees deal with family concerns.
- Minorities require different management styles: already companies are instituting training programs to help employees of different ethnic groups communicate.
- Immigrants require language accommodations: already, at Digital Equipment Corporation's Boston plant, 350 employees speak 19 languages. Company announcements are printed in English, Chinese, French, Spanish, Portuguese, Vietnamese, and Haitian Creole.

As the number of unskilled, uneducated workers grows, skilled workers are becoming more valuable. Companies are finding they must work harder to attract and retain them, as these desirable workers also place new demands on their employers:

- **Family first.** Having delayed marriage and family for their careers, many workers are now making up for lost time. They are leaving jobs that demand long hours, opting for part-time jobs and job-sharing. They are requesting flexible schedules that permit them to visit their children's teachers, take vacations, and attend school plays. And they are demanding flexible benefit packages that help them meet family needs.
- **Meaning *on* the job.** Today's skilled workers don't want jobs, they want careers. They want to be listened to and trusted.

They want the freedom to make decisions. They want flexibility and creativity, room to contribute, and room to grow.

- **Meaning *in* the job.** These workers want to be part of companies they believe in. They want to feel that their company is contributing solutions to the problems facing the world.

Can business rise to the challenges of the new work force? Successful ones will—by developing flexible management systems; by encouraging problem-solving and autonomy; by strengthering their communities to increase the pool of skilled employees; and by engaging in socially responsible behavior that attracts desirable workers. Nonprofit partnerships are one vehicle that will help companies respond to these human resource needs.

Challenge #4: The Rise of Niche Marketing and Advertising Clutter

In the good old days, when growth was the buzzword and new consumers were easy to find, mass marketing was a perfectly respectable—and reasonably efficient—way to expand market share. Companies offered products and services to broad market segments. By advertising on network TV, in mass-market magazines, and in daily newspapers, they could be fairly well assured that enough consumers would see their ads, want their products, and respond. Today this broad market strategy no longer works. Increasingly sophisticated consumers are demanding ever more specialized products. As a result, the sheer number of products has increased, but the market for each has become smaller and more specialized. Mass-market vehicles are now too expensive and reach too many of the ''wrong'' consumers to justify their cost.

Advertising clutter has also made it more difficult for a company to get its message heard. With sixteen thousand advertising messages bombarding consumers each day, how can you ensure that they'll hear yours?

How can companies market successfully in this climate? Public purpose partnerships can help by enabling companies to "micro-market": to reach small groups of consumers with similar needs and wants. Partnerships can help companies differentiate their products and services from the competition's by building strong associations between products and nonprofit causes. And they can help companies build long-term relationships with customers by promoting companies' long-term commitments to a cause.

Challenge #5: The Changing Role of Government

The government is scaling back numerous "lines of business." Welfare programs have been cut. Housing subsidies have declined. Eligibility for Medicaid has been tightened. In areas where government funds have remained stable, hardships have mounted, causing a net loss in support. The resulting problems are all too familiar: increasing poverty and homelessness, deteriorating infrastructures, failing school systems and health-care systems, rising devastation by drugs and crime.

In an effort to stem the loss of services, government is asking business to take up the slack—and business is responding. It is venturing into issues such as education, substance abuse, and AIDS education and care by supporting workplace and community programs. It is contracting with federal and state agencies to perform government functions, such as operating prisons, providing mail service, and collecting garbage. It is forming partnerships with nonprofit agencies to strengthen communities through job training programs and economic development.

The cutback in government services has created a new role for business. But can business afford to play it? Enlightened companies believe they have no choice. They know that investment in schools will produce qualified employees. They know that investment in the arts will help make communities better places to live and work. They know that investment in social services will help keep the United States competitive. They also know that nonprofit partnerships are one tool that can help them make these investments efficiently and effectively.

Who Can Profit at a Time Like This?

Good question. Not business as we knew it, certainly. The old strategies, the old ways of thinking and operating just don't work anymore. Whereas once upon a time a business was responsible primarily to stockholders, today a business is responsible to stakeholders—to the customers, the employees, the suppliers, the shareholders, the government, the neighborhood, the environment—to all the people and places that business affects.

It's a tall order for a company that just wants to make and sell its widgets. But companies that fail to fill that order won't survive. Companies that want to fill the order will find partnerships with nonprofits a powerful instrument for building long-term profitability and survival.

CHAPTER 4

Potential Problems—and How to Avoid Them

Is Sprint doing this to get your business? What difference does it make? We're doing it.

—Candice Bergen, in a TV commercial advertising U.S. Sprint's cause-related marketing campaign benefiting environmental organizations

In mid-1991 U.S. Sprint unveiled a series of television commercials featuring Candice Bergen. Gazing out at the viewer, the beautiful film and TV star announced that a portion of all customer payments to Sprint for long-distance telephone service would be donated to a number of environmental organizations. "Why are we doing this?" Bergen asked. She answered her own question with the quote above. An equally good question is: why did the commercial's writers feel they had to include that question and answer in the spot? According to David Riemer, of J. Walter Thompson, San Francisco, the ad agency that created the commercial, the line was written to satisfy skeptics—to speak to cynical consumers who believe that partnerships between corporations and nonprofits have nothing to do with helping a worthy cause and everything to do with generating sales. The fact that the agency believed it needed to address that sentiment so directly is a telling indication of the number of people who see public purpose partnerships in that negative light.

In many ways, this is not surprising. Since the mid-1980s hundreds of thousands of businesses have tied sales promotions to nonprofit causes. Everything from toasters to teddy bears has been sold "to benefit" a worthy cause. How could consumers not become at least a little cynical?

That cynicism is no reason to avoid partnerships. Well-planned campaigns that truly benefit both partners receive praise rather than criticism. But as you consider entering into a public purpose partnership, you should be aware of the criticisms some campaigns have received. It will help you design your own partnership so that it is honest, mutually beneficial, and successful.

Using a Nonprofit

The biggest criticism launched at public purpose partnerships is that corporations that establish them are using nonprofits for their own gain. This is a serious accusation. In our society nonprofits are held in high esteem precisely because they are not commercial—because they exist for the public good and not for the benefit of individuals. We invest nonprofits with a high degree of "purity," and using a nonprofit for commercial purposes violates that purity. Companies that do it risk harming their image. Nonprofits that allow it run the same risk.

Witness the case of Philip Morris and the Bill of Rights. In 1989 the cigarette manufacturer announced it was spending $60 million to celebrate the 200th anniversary of the signing of the Bill of Rights. The celebration would include a traveling exhibition which would take the document to all fifty states, and an ad campaign touting America's political freedoms. Assisting the company in this endeavor—for the sum of $600,000—was the National Archives, repository of the document and of other historical materials used in the campaign.

No sooner did the first ad (a view of the Capitol rotunda with voices of former presidents and other leaders reading from the Bill of Rights, followed by the Philip Morris logo) hit the airwaves than a hue and cry erupted from consumers and health organizations, decrying the campaign as a sleazy attempt to use a national symbol to reinforce the company's own campaign for smokers' rights. As the Bill of Rights exhibition toured the country, antismoking groups appeared on the evening news picketing the installation at almost every stop. From a public relations standpoint, the campaign was a disaster. The National Archives didn't fare much better. It, too, was criticized, for having allowed itself to be "bought" for so commercial a venture.

Campaigns featuring less symbolic causes have also drawn scorn from consumers. After the San Francisco earthquake in 1989, Burger King announced that it would give $.25 to the Red Cross to aid earthquake victims each time someone ordered its new BK Double burger. That might have been fine had the company not begun promoting the burger several weeks earlier. The campaign was perceived by many as a blatant attempt to capitalize on a disaster in order to promote a new product. The campaign raised $3 million in its first two weeks— a hefty sum for people very much in need—but not without angering some consumers.

"Buying" a Nonprofit

A second criticism lobbed at public purpose partnerships is that participating nonprofits will lose their programmatic independence, becoming pawns of their corporate partners. This concern is understandable. At a time of declining government grants, nonprofits' need for money is at an all-time high. In their desire to attract corporate funds, the temptation is real to tailor what they do to corporate interests. Corporations, perceiving the marketing potential involved, are not shy about asking for favors.

We see this clearly in the case of museums. Where once corporate donors to museums were satisfied to get their names on a panel next to the exhibition title, today's exhibition sponsors are requesting—and sometimes getting—a lot more. The Formica Corporation, for instance, organized, curated, and helped underwrite several exhibits that visited museums around the country. The shows featured works made with the company's materials. Tiffany & Company initiated and paid for exhibits showcasing its jewelry and silver which visited the Field Museum of Natural History in Chicago and the Museum of Fine Arts in Boston. Other companies have made similar arrangements. Should museums accept these company-initiated shows? Or do they reflect a bending of museum standards in order to attract sponsors and make money?

Environmental groups, too, have been accused of selling out to corporate interests. The World Wildlife Fund, the National Wildlife Federation, and the Audubon Society have all received large grants from corporations whose environmental records are poor. The agencies claim that they can remain objective regardless of who's paying the bills. But skeptics are not so sure. The corporate sugar daddies don't come out smelling like roses, either. Chevron, Mobil, Exxon, and other companies have been accused of buying off their adversaries by funding the groups that oppose their environmental practices.

Are the nonprofits being bought? Are the corporations buying—or merely helping? Nobody knows for sure, but even the suspicion can damage reputations.

The Loss of Traditional Philanthropy?

A third criticism leveled at public purpose partnerships is that they will jeopardize traditional, "pure" philanthropy. If corporations can get something in exchange for their dollars, will they continue to give money with no quid pro quo? Evidence suggests they will. Purely philanthropic corporate donations have actually risen since the late 1980s, when partnerships first began to gather steam.

If anything, the rise of partnerships has opened up more corporate money for nonprofits, since nonprofits can now tap corporate marketing as well as philanthropic budgets. A 1987 survey conducted by Sheridan and Associates for the Independent Sector, an association of foundations and nonprofit organizations, revealed that companies that had entered into nonprofit partnerships kept their philanthropic budgets and their partnership budgets separate, and that partnership activities had had no impact on their corporate giving. A few companies actually reported that their partnership programs had resulted in larger donations to their nonprofit partners because of the additional attention they received.

A related concern is that partnership activities will cause a decline in individual contributions. If people believe they've contributed to a cause by buying a product or attending an event, will they still write a check when a solicitation letter comes in the mail? Again, evidence suggests this is not a problem. Like corporate contributions, individual donations have steadily risen since the mid-1980s. This shouldn't come as a surprise, since one of the biggest goals of partnership campaigns is to draw attention to the needs of nonprofits and recruit new donors. Successful campaigns should increase donations, not siphon them away.

Will Only "Sexy" Nonprofits Benefit?

In the early days of public purpose partnerships a common criticism was that corporations would choose as their partners only "sexy" or "mediagenic" nonprofits. Critics feared that while these organizations might benefit greatly from the strategy, the majority of agencies would be left out. Causes such as battered women, homeless people, and people with AIDS would be too depressing to make good partnerships. Experience has shown this to be untrue. Some of the biggest and best-publicized partnerships have targeted precisely those groups. Hands Across America, for example, a 1986 made-for-TV mega-event, cajoled hundreds of thousands of people into joining hands in a coast-to-coast human chain to raise money for the homeless. Corporations shelled out millions of dollars in cash and in-kind donations. In a 1987 campaign, called Shelter Aid, Johnson & Johnson raised more than $1.5 million for battered women's shelters. The campaign was the company's most successful promotion ever.

One truth about public purpose partnerships seems to be that virtually any kind of cause will work because every cause and every nonprofit appeals to a particular audience. Johnson & Johnson chose battered women because the company believed that would appeal to its target market, women. Levi Strauss & Co. gives money to AIDS projects in part because the corporation knows that many of its young urban customers feel strongly about the issue. First Interstate Bank of California created a credit card for the Foundation for Wild Sheep in which a percentage of every purchase made with the card was given to the Foundation because even that esoteric organization had a membership base worth pursuing. The surprise to early critics of public purpose partnerships is that every cause has a following. For companies that want to attract that following, partnerships can be an effective vehicle.

Fostering Nonprofit Dependence

Yet another concern sometimes voiced by critics of the strategy is that nonprofits will become dependent on their corporate partners for money and will suffer once a partnership ends. This criticism doesn't carry a lot of weight. No manager of a nonprofit going into a campaign thinks the campaign will last forever. He or she knows the money generated will supplement, rather than replace, existing funds.

Nonetheless, companies that want to address this concern can help their nonprofit partners develop long-term strategies for increasing their revenues. They can actively recruit donors among their own employees and customers. They can lend their marketing staffs to help their partners develop fund-raising campaigns. They can help their partners develop long-range plans that include new sources of income.

Cash is just one thing a corporation has to offer a nonprofit partner. Marketing and managerial support can be every bit as helpful in the long run. In fact, more than any cash donation, partnerships have the potential to make nonprofits *independent* and *self-reliant*.

Avoiding Criticism

So how can companies engaging in partnerships avoid criticism? The answer is simple: be sincere. If your campaign is honorable in intent, it will be honorably perceived. If you genuinely support your partner—if your campaign does as much for the nonprofit as it does for you—the public will believe you mean it.

Body Shop International is a retailer of natural, cruelty-free cosmetics, widely recognized for its socially responsible business practices. Posters and literature in Body Shop stores promote environmental causes. Sales people are given time off to volunteer. The company builds plants in depressed areas to stimulate local economies. Body Shop's 50 percent annual growth in the last decade is largely attributed to its social policies. Anita Roddick, Body Shop founder, has been a vocal advocate of corporations adopting social causes, and an equally strong critic of companies that do so insincerely. She warns: "[Consumers] can sniff out integrity and sniff out dishonesty, and know instinctively what is junk and what is true. They can spot arrogant jargon."

In fact, the campaigns that backfire are the ones that are designed strictly as sales promotions. See our ad! Buy our product! Help support our cause! The trouble is, in three short months the campaign is over and the cause is never mentioned again. How committed can that company be?

The campaigns that work are the ones in which the company truly supports the cause—and shows it time and time again. The company makes donations. It lends employees. It touts the cause in its ads. Sure, it invites the public to help by purchasing products or attending events. But it does an equal amount on its own. Those are partnerships you can believe in.

So if you want to establish a partnership—and remain above reproach—take it seriously. Be sincere. Pick a cause you believe in. Then find as many ways as possible to express that belief. Communicate your partner's message in your ads. Make in-kind donations. Encourage employees to volunteer. Create a long-term partnership in which you remind the public over and over of your commitment. If you believe in your partnership, the public will believe in it, too.

The fact is, corporations are in a powerful position to help nonprofits—by giving them cash, by exposing them to the public, by helping get their message out, by helping them find new donors. But the onus is on both partners to make sure the campaign works. The nonprofit must make sure that it is not bought or exploited. The corporation must believe that by supporting its partner, it supports its own goals.

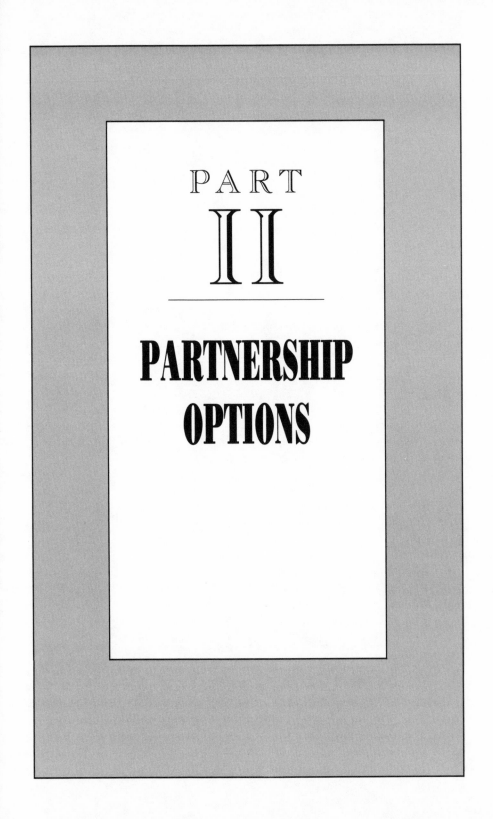

PART

II

PARTNERSHIP OPTIONS

CHAPTER 5

Strategic Philanthropy

Can corporate philanthropy be an effective marketing tool? You bet!

—C. R. Hogan, Jr., manager of corporate contributions,
United Technologies Corporation
Hartford, CT

It's tempting to think of strategic philanthropy as a new phenomenon. Actually, only the name is new. The practice of using philanthropic dollars to buy benefits for a company dates to the 1800s.

America's railroad barons first raised philanthropy to a strategic art. These early industrialists were the primary benefactors of the YMCA—not because they believed in the Y's programs, but because they needed cheap housing for their railroad crews. Shrewdly, they saw the benefit of serving the community *and* their business interests with one project.

Their practice established a precedent that lasted for the next fifty years. In fact, it was mandated by corporate law, which held that a company's donations must directly benefit its stockholders. This only changed in 1954 when the New Jersey Supreme Court ruled that a publicly held business could make charitable donations that did not produce income for stockholders. That decision triggered a trend in the opposite direction. For three subsequent decades, corporations tended to give donations to organizations far removed from their fields of business to avoid the appearance of gain.

They didn't forgo intangible benefits, however. Throughout those decades most corporations strategically spent philanthropic dollars on community programs. These expenditures served two purposes. They strengthened community resources, making the community a better place to recruit employees and raise a family—in short, to run a company. Equally important, they bought the goodwill of employees, customers, and government officials.

Other companies strategically spent philanthropic dollars on cultural events with specifically targeted payoffs. When United Technologies Corporation, for example, wanted to build its business in the Middle East, it sponsored a Smithsonian exhibition of Islamic art. Why? The exhibition built important contacts for the company in Saudi Arabia, facilitating the company's entry into that market. Another example: since 1940, Texaco has sponsored broadcasts of the Metropolitan Opera. Why such a long association? Because the company has more than twice its normal market share among motorists who regularly listen to opera.

Recently, the trend toward strategic philanthropy has been picking up steam. Given the times, that's hardly surprising. With a tight economy and tighter budgets, companies are under increased pressure to justify all expenses. If contributions can be targeted to causes that also help the bottom line, so much the better: they are easier to sell to management and to shareholders.

New Goals for Giving

As more and more companies adopt strategic giving, their uses for the strategy become broader and more sophisticated. Shrewd business leaders have recognized its power to support a variety of corporate goals.

On Saturday afternoon, December 7, 1940, Americans turned on their radios to hear a live broadcast of the Metropolitan Opera performing *Le Nozze di Figaro* sponsored by Texaco. This historic broadcast inaugurated a tradition that is still going strong.

Over the past 50 years, Texaco has been proud to bring you the immortal stars of the Met, the most distinguished productions in opera history and the greatest music ever composed. Tune in as Texaco and the Metropolitan Opera begin their second half-century of live radio broadcasts.

This advertisement is reprinted with permission of Texaco Inc.

Business Development

Companies are using philanthropic dollars to open doors to new lines of business.

- The Bristol-Myers Squibb Foundation, like most drug company foundations, gives money to universities to support research that may eventually benefit the company.
- When United Technologies wanted to cement its position as one of the leading aerospace companies doing business in France, it sponsored another Smithsonian exhibition, this one on French landscape painting. The exhibition opened at the National Gallery in Washington, D.C., then moved to Paris, where the opening was attended by officials of the French government who were in a position to help the company.

Human Resources

Companies are using philanthropic dollars to buy programs that respond to the needs of their present employees, and to fund programs that will help create better employees in the future.

- Stride Rite corporation in Cambridge, Massachusetts, uses money from its corporate foundation (the Stride Rite Charitable Foundation) to subsidize tuition at its two on-site day-care centers. Stride Rite is one of only about 200 U.S. companies to offer on-site day care, and the only one to offer an intergenerational center that serves both children and elderly relatives of employees. Arnold Hiatt, Stride Rite CEO, believes the two centers actually save the children's shoe manufacturer $22,000 per employee by helping it retain high-quality workers and avoid the cost of training replacements.
- Dayton Hudson Corporation was having a hard time recruiting qualified entry-level employees for its department stores—so it used philanthropic dollars to create its own job training program. The Job-Plus program recruits teenage mothers on welfare and trains them in basic childcare, communications and job search skills that will help

them in the workplace as well as in life. It then places them in jobs in Dayton's stores.

• Pacific Telesis is making an even longer-term investment in employee development. After testing 3,500 people for entry-level jobs and finding that only 1 in 20 passed, the company decided to plow $2 million into a five-year program to reform California's elementary schools. Education for the Future funds classroom experiments in new methods of education. State legislators and educators, as well as local parents and administrators, are PacTel's partners in the program.

Marketing

Companies use philanthropic dollars to reinforce image and build customer loyalty.

• For years, Mobil has sponsored programs on public television because it strengthened the company's image with educated consumers. In fact, the sponsorship strengthened Mobil's image so much that the company consistently gets letters thanking it for a PBS Shakespeare series funded by its competitor.

• McDonald's funds the Ronald McDonald Houses for families of children in hospitals because the program builds loyalty with its own family of customers.

• Within its corporate giving department, the Adolph Coors Company has three initiatives, specifically targeting three populations: African Americans, women, and Hispanics. Each year the company gives a predetermined amount of money to nonprofit causes that appeal to each of those groups, because it knows that support of minority causes will help it build business with those consumers.

A New Game Plan, Too

Companies that are using philanthropy as a strategic tool have made some fundamental changes in the way they arrive at funding decisions. Gone are the days when the interest of a chief executive was all it took to get a check for a favorite cause. Companies that practice enlightened self-interest are putting sophisticated systems in place to guide their philanthropic decisions.

Funding Criteria

Obviously, the funding criteria for grants have changed. Whereas "pure" philanthropic decisions were generally guided by the need for programs and the merit of applicants, strategic philanthropy in decisions employ a broader set of measures. These include a company's marketing, human resources, and business development goals, as well as the interests of its range of constituents. The appeal of a program to a company's customers, employees, shareholders, and community is considered as the company makes a funding decision.

Who Decides

Companies that practice "pure" philanthropy generally leave funding decisions to their corporate giving staffs. Strategic givers bring a broader range of people into the decision:

- Human resources staff are consulted about employee concerns, work-force development issues, and other areas of need that might be served by a corporate gift.
- Marketing staff are asked about the company's marketing goals: are there target populations that might be served through a donation?
- Public relations staff are asked how a gift could help the company achieve PR goals in the community.
- Community relations staff are asked what community problems might be targeted.
- Business development officers, government relations specialists, and shareholder relations staff may also be brought in to contribute to the decision.

Goals

The goal of "pure" philanthropy is relatively simple: to benefit the recipient agencies. The goals of strategic philanthropy are more complex: to produce a variety of returns to the corporation. To guarantee those returns, some strategic givers outline the goals of their gifts in measurable terms: 25 percent of employees will participate in the program; all major local media will pick up the story; two of the five research projects will be on subjects we pick; we will have two opening parties with guests of our choosing; and so on. Goals are established by all the relevant players.

Some corporations carry out formal evaluations after the fact to see if their goals were met. They treat their gifts like business expenses, measuring the results as they would in any business program.

Funding Impact

Strategic givers want their donations to have an impact on the company; they also want them to have an impact on the world. As a result, the old "smorgasbord" approach of donating small sums to many disparate groups has given way to much more targeted grant-making. Strategic givers tend to pick one or two areas in which to make grants—typically areas with a direct impact on their community or on their business—and spend larger sums in those areas. Hence we see insurance companies targeting AIDS education and AIDS research; bookstores targeting illiteracy; food processing companies targeting food banks and soup kitchens.

Recognition

"Pure" philanthropists often give grants anonymously or with little fanfare. Not so strategic givers, who generally want the greatest possible exposure for their gifts. After all, public recognition is an important element of the strategy. Since most gifts are designed to build goodwill, the more people who know, the better. In fact, a public relations campaign is often used to support the program.

The Shape of Things to Come?

Will more companies adopt strategic giving in the future? Undoubtedly. With companies under increasing pressure to do more with less, the strategy is too effective to ignore. In 1988, the Daniel Yankelovich Group, a New York market research firm, surveyed 225 chief executives of major corporations and 100 executives described as "next generation CEOs" in a study for The Council on Foundations. Seventy-one percent felt that a company *must* determine the benefits to the business of each cause it supports. The next generation CEOs were particularly adamant about the need to emphasize corporate self-interest in giving policy. Another indication that the trend is here to stay is the number of specialty companies that have sprung up in the past three to four years just to support strategic giving. These companies consult with corporations, foundations, and individuals on methods for getting the maximum return from their charitable gifts. They help target social concerns that match business needs, and then build customized giving strategies.

But Is It Philanthropy?

The rise of strategic philanthropy raises a lot of questions. For instance, is it really philanthropy, or is it really business-building disguised as a tax-deductible contribution? Are corporate philanthropists being co-opted by their colleagues in marketing and corporate communications? Are some nonprofits endangered by this trend? And is "pure" philanthropy dying? Let's take these questions one at a time.

Is It Really Philanthropy?

Yes. Emphatically. On the most fundamental level it is philanthropy because the money comes from the corporate foundation and must meet IRS guidelines for its use. Money for business partnerships with nonprofits comes from the business side of the ledger. On a more important level it is philanthropy because of its goal. A corporation's primary goal in strategic philanthropy is to benefit a nonprofit. Its primary goal in a business partnership is to benefit the corporation. This is a very important difference. Corporations give money to art museums because they know art museums need support. They fund programs in public schools because government funds are inadequate. *That corporate benefits are tied to those goals does not diminish their philanthropic objectives.*

If business benefits were the primary goal, corporations would be better off funding the programs with money from their business budgets. Those budgets are larger; they have fewer strings attached; and business expenses are just as tax-deductible as philanthropic expenditures. There is no advantage to using philanthropic dollars to fund business-building programs. In fact, most corporate foundations specifically prohibit it.

Are Corporate Philanthropists Being Co-opted by Marketers?

Not the smart ones! Shrewd corporate givers get as much as they give when they work with colleagues in marketing. In exchange for involving the marketers in their philanthropic decisions, they snare marketing resources for their grant recipients. Instead of just writing a check to a nonprofit, they offer the agency a full-blown publicity campaign. This is manna to nonprofits, whose missions involve getting the word out to the public about what they are doing. Frequently corporate givers tap other corporate resources as well. They work with human relations to recruit employee volunteers. They set up employee donation programs. They include information about the nonprofit in their customer mailings. In fact, for all these reasons, nonprofits are better served by strategic philanthropy than they are by simply receiving a check. Which brings up the next question.

Are Nonprofits Endangered by This Trend?

No. For all the reasons above, nonprofits benefit from this trend. Strategic philanthropy is not just strategic for the corporation. It is equally strategic for the nonprofit because it mobilizes a variety of corporate resources to carry out the agency's mission. It is the vehicle of choice for companies that seriously want to make a difference.

Is "Pure" Philanthropy Dying?

Even the most ardent practitioners of strategic philanthropy still engage in "pure" philanthropy as well. As long as United Way exists, as long as chief executives have a say, companies will still give money to worthy causes. The tradition of "pure" philanthropy is too ingrained in our culture to peter out, no matter how tight money gets.

In fact, most companies that practice strategic philanthropy do so with only a small number of their grant recipients, if only because working strategically with a partner takes more time and effort than writing a check. Staff people need to carefully select the partner; orchestrate an event or campaign; and work with the partner as they do it. It's a time-consuming process. So don't look for "pure" philanthropy to die out soon. Writing a check will always be the quickest and easiest way to benefit a nonprofit. It's just not always the most effective.

CHAPTER 6

Cause-Related Marketing

I need garbage bags anyway. Why not spend my money helping some organization at the same time?

—Los Angeles shopper

For the consumer, cause-related marketing is a simple, painless way to ease the conscience.

—Mava Heffler, former director of sales promotion, Johnson & Johnson

If there is such a thing as a win-win-win proposition, cause-related marketing (CRM) is it. Corporations earn money and goodwill. Non-profits gain money and exposure. And consumers get to spend money and feel good about it. In cause-related marketing, capitalism has actually become a philanthropic tool.

CRM needs little introduction. Only a Rip Van Winkle could have missed the flurry of cents-off coupons tied to charities that sprouted on everything from cereal to toilet tissue during the late 1980s. In fact, the strategy became so ubiquitous that by the early 1990s many large marketers believed it had lost its appeal and eliminated or reduced their CRM campaigns. But today CRM has made a comeback.

The number—and range—of companies practicing it has grown dramatically, with many smaller companies adopting the strategy in strictly local campaigns. As a technique of generating sales for companies and revenue for nonprofits, the strategy is unassailable. The question now is not whether or not to do CRM—but how to do it well.

Defining Terms

Cause-related marketing has come to mean so many things over the years that it bears defining. In CRM, a corporation and a nonprofit enter a joint promotional campaign. Consumers are encouraged to purchase the corporation's products, knowing that a percentage of each sale will go to the nonprofit. Most often this is done through the use of cents-off coupons: for each coupon redeemed, the corporation donates a fixed amount to the nonprofit, frequently up to a preestablished ceiling. By tapping consumer interest in a worthy cause, corporations are generally able to increase sales; they also generate goodwill. Nonprofits benefit by raising money, and by having their name and message widely broadcast.

Cause-related marketing is just that: marketing. It happens to have a philanthropic result, but *its primary purpose is sales*. It requires a consumer *to buy a company's product or service* in order to benefit the cause. A corporation sponsoring a rock concert that benefits a nonprofit, therefore, is not engaging in CRM. Nor is a company that gives its product or service free to a nonprofit organization. Those companies are engaged in public purpose partnerships, yes—but they're not engaged in CRM.

How It All Began

CRM burst onto the national scene in 1983 when American Express, in a highly visible $6-million advertising campaign, offered during a three-month period to give a percentage of each purchase made with an American Express card, a percentage of each AmEx "travel package" over $500, a percentage of sales of American Express Travelers' Cheques, and a percentage of each new card application, to the Statue of Liberty–Ellis Island restoration fund. The results of the campaign made marketing history. AmEx card use rose 28 percent; new card applications rose 17 percent; and the campaign raised $1.7 million for the Statue of Liberty and Ellis Island. The campaign was so successful, in fact, that most people thought American Express was an official sponsor of the statue restoration, although the company had never actually paid to be one.

That this campaign was so successful is not surprising. American Express had actually been practicing CRM since 1981, when it developed the concept in response to three clearly defined marketing goals: to convince consumers to acquire and use AmEx charge cards; to convince more businesses to accept the cards; and to find newsworthy ways of doing it.

The company was also aware of growing demand for corporations to be socially responsible—to give back to the communities in which they did business. Could "giving back to the community" somehow be linked to card purchases and card use? Could it become the newsworthy marketing tool AmEx wanted? As the company's managers pondered the possibilities, they realized that they had more to give a community than money. Their ability to create powerful promotional campaigns could be extremely beneficial to nonprofit organizations with small budgets but big messages to get out.

From this mulling of multiple needs came the strategy. In selected markets—communities where the company wanted to expand—American Express tied its business to an arts group—an orchestra, a theater, a museum—something it knew would interest card holders. Large advertising campaigns urged consumers to shop, dine, and travel using the American Express card, because every purchase would benefit the selected organization. The ads also touted the strengths of the arts groups, giving them significant exposure.

The campaigns worked. In every one, card use rose and local media picked up the story, generating the publicity the company wanted. The arts groups received unrestricted income, as well as tremendous public exposure. Some even received benefits beyond those anticipated, as donations, memberships, and business connections increased.

In 1983, American Express made the Statue of Liberty the first *national* CRM campaign, and since then thousands of similar partnerships have been spawned between consumer-oriented corporations and nonprofits. Partners have included large national organizations like the Red Cross and MasterCard, as well as small-town social service agencies working with local retailers. In some instances nonprofits have approached corporations to codevelop a campaign; more often corporations have sought out nonprofits. Some of the larger, nationally known nonprofits have received so many requests for partnerships that they have created full-time staff positions to develop and manage CRM programs. The added staff expense is well worth it, since Big Brothers Big Sisters, the Special Olympics, the American Cancer Society, and the American Heart Association have all raised millions of dollars through CRM campaigns. Smaller nonprofits have raised smaller amounts—generally less than 10 percent of their annual income—but the secondary benefits of exposure, public education, and recruitment of members, volunteers, and new donors all add to the campaigns' value.

On the corporate side, responses have been equally positive. Fred Wilkinson, senior vice president for corporate initiatives at American Express, says the company's cause-related marketing programs have produced results "at least as good as, and frequently better than" conventional marketing programs. Texize Division of Dow Consumer Products Company, manufacturer of household cleaners, after a CRM campaign with the National Crime Prevention Council, announced it had had its best quarter ever. Scott Paper Company's CRM campaign for Ronald McDonald Houses was the most successful sales promotion in Scott history. Johnson & Johnson called its CRM campaign, Shelter Aid, its most successful promotion ever.

Thousands of smaller companies have also found CRM campaigns extremely effective at generating sales and consumer interest. They have helped companies strengthen their image as good community citizens. And they have had a residual effect on company employees: sales forces, franchisees, and plant and office workers have all responded with interest, pride, and improved morale to CRM efforts.

Using CRM for a Variety of Marketing Needs

For a fairly simple strategy, CRM is remarkably flexible. It can be tailored to a company's specific marketing needs. Here are the ways some companies have used the strategy.

Boosting a Single Brand

Numerous companies have used CRM to boost sales of a single brand. By linking the brand with a nonprofit, they have created or reinforced its image; have gained the attention of a particular audience; or have encouraged consumers to give the brand a try. For example, Kimberly-Clark wanted more mothers to buy Huggies diapers. How to get their attention? The company partnered Children's Miracle Network in a CRM campaign to raise money for children's hospitals. The campaign tugged the heartstrings of exactly the market Kimberly-Clark wanted, *and* built an association between Huggies and children's doctors. Who better to vouch for a diaper's quality?

Pumping an Entire Product Line

Rather than focusing on a single brand, some companies use CRM to promote an entire product line. The benefit: marketing efficiency, promoting several products in one campaign. The caveat: all the products must logically relate to the cause and the nonprofit. For example, Johnson & Johnson wanted to reinforce the quality and breadth of its line of first-aid products. What is the first name in first aid? The Red Cross. So Johnson & Johnson created an across-the-line partnership: each time a consumer redeemed a coupon for Band-Aids, gauze pads, or other first-aid item, the company gave a percentage of the sale to the Red Cross. The obvious connection between the product line and the nonprofit made the campaign work.

Reinforcing a Company's Image

Some companies have used CRM to boost or reinforce their corporate image by tying virtually all their brands to a cause. This can be tricky to pull off, since it requires a cause and a nonprofit that relate strongly to all the brands. Johnson & Johnson was able to do it because the company makes a wide variety of products, but all are marketed to the same consumers: women.

In 1987 Johnson & Johnson created a nine-brand CRM campaign around the cause of battered women. The Shelter Aid campaign raised money to establish and staff the first year of a toll-free hotline for abused women, and donated money to a nationwide network of battered women's shelters. Four Johnson & Johnson business units joined in the campaign, which featured products ranging from baby shampoo to tampons. The campaign netted more than $1 million for the hotline and shelters and resulted in significant market share increases for the participating brands. The StayFree line of feminine hygiene products experienced a dramatic increase in sales.

Cause-Related Marketing with a Twist

No sooner had the CRM bug bitten marketers nationwide than companies began coming up with variations. It seemed almost anything could be tied into a donation to a nonprofit—with positive results all around.

Letting the Customer Pick the Cause

Most CRM campaigns ask consumers to buy into a preestablished partnership. However, a few companies have strategically not preselected a nonprofit partner, instead letting their customers pick the cause.

On a national level this was done successfully by MasterCard in a 1987 campaign called Choose to Make a Difference. Each time customers used MasterCard, the company donated money to one of six national nonprofits: the American Heart Association, Mothers Against Drunk Driving, the National Committee for Prevention of Child Abuse, the Muscular Dystrophy Association, the National Association on Drug Abuse Problems, and AMC Cancer Research Centers. The choice to include six nonprofits was made in response to market research. Studies had shown that baby boomers wanted to give to charity, but they didn't want to feel the sting. They also wanted to decide which charities they supported. So MasterCard designed its campaign accordingly, polling consumers to learn which charities were of greatest interest to them. MasterCard built its campaign around the "winners" and around consumers' ability to choose between them.

Did market research pay off? It did. The campaign raised $2.8 million for the six charities—and boosted MasterCard use by 19 percent. According to consumer surveys, it also gave MasterCard a better image than VISA for the first time ever.

Letting the consumer pick the cause has also been successful on a much smaller, local level. Ukrop's Super Markets of Richmond, Virginia, donates 10 percent of its pretax profits to charity, but it lets its customers pick the charities. From June to September every year, Ukrop's prints its cash-register receipts on gold paper. Customers are encouraged to give their receipts to the local charities of their choice. The charities then return the receipts to Ukrop's, which gives each charity 2 percent of the face value (excluding sales tax). About 40 percent of all receipts are redeemed during the promotion, which generates increased business for the store. Ukrop's wanted to let its customers vote on charitable donations, and its marketing managers believe the program works. "If we didn't think that we were coming out with more benefits than costs, we wouldn't continue it," said Carol Beth Spivey, marketing and communications coordinator for Ukrop's. "We're just nuts about the program."

Perhaps the ultimate in letting the customer pick the cause is a 1990 strategy devised by Cunard Lines. Cunard has long offered cruise packages to groups, but recently discovered a new way of boosting its group tour business. In full-page ads, the company touts the benefits of a Cunard cruise as a fund-raiser for charitable organizations, offering to donate a portion of the fares to any organization that books a group package. To the partners' mutual advantage, the company also offers to help the organization promote the trip to members.

Linking CRM with a Special Event

Linking a cause-related marketing campaign with a special event can be extremely effective for several reasons. It draws increased attention to the campaign. It provides additional benefit to the non-profit. And it reinforces the company's connection with the cause. This last is particularly important as the number of CRM campaigns grows. Companies doing CRM need to let the public know that their commitment to the cause is real and continuing—not just a strategy for winning sales.

General Foods did this successfully in a 1985 partnership with Mothers Against Drunk Drivers (MADD). The company wanted to regain market share and shelf space for Tang, its powdered orange juice. Since mothers are the major purchasers of orange juice, General Foods approached MADD with an idea for a combined special event and CRM campaign. The company distributed cents-off coupons promising to give $.10 to MADD for each Tang proof-of-purchase seal redeemed during a four-month period, up to $100,000. To call attention to the offer—and to MADD's cause—General Foods sponsored the Tang March Across America, an event in which MADD chapters in each city organized walkers who collected pledges for the cause. Each city's walk ended with a high-visibility public celebration hosted by General Foods.

The combined campaign was powerful. The CRM aspect worked directly on Tang sales nationwide. The march extended the campaign and gave it a strong presence in each city. The culminating public celebration reinvigorated the campaign one more time, reminding consumers about the importance of the issue and of General Foods' efforts on its behalf. When the campaign ended, MADD had collected $100,000 in donations; warehouse shipments of Tang had increased 13 percent; and the brand had regained valuable shelf space it had lost the previous year.

Strengthening CRM with a Premium

Offering a premium item as part of a CRM campaign provides several enhancements. It gives consumers a lasting reminder of your partnership. It gives them one more way to support the cause. And it gives them one more way to do business with your company.

Georgia-Pacific, maker of MD toilet tissues, carried out a combined CRM and premium campaign with the World Wildlife Fund (WWF) in 1987. In national ads, MD advertised its support of WWF's mission and invited consumers to help support the fund by redeeming a cents-off coupon. In a conventional CRM campaign, Georgia-Pacific gave $.05 to WWF for every coupon redeemed, up to a ceiling of $20,000. But then the manufacturer added a twist: with two proof-of-purchase seals from MD tissues and $11.15, consumers could purchase a WWF plush toy at a savings of $7 to $10. For each toy purchased, Georgia-Pacific promised to send $1 to WWF.

The premium addition enhanced the campaign in several ways. It promoted sales of the product by providing an additional incentive to buy. It provided additional income to WWF, which first sold the plush toys to Georgia-Pacific and then collected $1 per toy ordered. And it put the WWF message into every home, on a tag attached to the toy.

CRM with Proof-of-Purchase Seals

Rather than tie donations to cents-off coupons, some companies trigger donations with proof-of-purchase seals. The effect is the same, since consumers have to buy the product to benefit the nonprofit. However, the fact that proof-of-purchase seals linger after the purchase creates opportunities for innovative campaigns. Scott Paper Company, for example, uses this strategy in a continuing campaign called Learning Tools for Schools. Parents and students are invited to bring Scott proof-of-purchase seals to their schools, which can trade them in for educational equipment. To promote the program, Scott sends letters to elementary schools inviting them to participate. Then it helps them pitch the program to parents and students. Schools can redeem the seals for everything from books to Apple computers.

CRM for All Kinds of Companies

The majority of companies using CRM campaigns are manufacturers of packaged goods—with good reason. For these companies, coupon redemption is a traditional sales promotion technique. The addition of the nonprofit partner is merely a twist on an established practice. Coupons are distributed through the mail, through newspaper inserts, in magazine ads, and in point-of-purchase displays. However, these are not the only companies to successfully use this strategy. Numerous other kinds of corporations have also benefited by linking business with charitable donations:

- **Magazines:** Several magazines have used CRM campaigns to raise their advertising revenue while helping a worthy cause. *Mirabella* told its advertisers that for every ad page in its first anniversary issue, $1,000 would go to one of four charities, including an AIDS foundation and a literacy group. The magazine raised $82,000 for the nonprofits—and upped the number of ad pages in that issue.
- **Mailing Lists:** First Mail International, a mailing list company, used CRM to entice people to answer its consumer preferences survey. The company promised to give $1 to Easter Seals "in your name" to consumers who answered its forty-nine–question mail-in survey.
- **Restaurants:** Hershey Foods used CRM to create a sweet deal for its chain of Friendly's restaurants. Friendly's offered a coupon book worth $5.50 and two free ice cream cones to any customer who came into the store and donated $1 to Easter Seals. The result: $4 million for Easter Seals; sales and traffic gains for Friendly's.
- **Airlines:** Continental Airlines wanted to boost traffic at its Denver hub during the 1989 holiday season. So the airline undertook a CRM-type campaign to benefit Colorado's homeless. In full-page newspaper ads, Continental advertised that during the month of December, it would sell $50 discount airfare certificates for $25. Money earned from the certificates would be given to Father Woody, a Den-

ver pastor much acclaimed for his work with street people. For every certificate actually used, the airline promised to give another $10 to the cause. The promotion generated significant income for Father Woody. It also boosted traffic and helped smooth a bumpy image for the airline.

• **Banks:** Some people might draw the line at religion—but not Huntington National Bank. The Columbus, Ohio, bank offers financial services at local churches. It's part of a classic CRM effort to attract new customers. A member of the congregation is trained by the bank as a part-time employee to help churchgoers with loans and account paperwork during regular church hours. Each time a customer opens an account or takes out a loan, the church gets from $15 to $250, depending on the size and scope of the transaction. For the bank it's a way to build business in low-to-moderate-income neighborhoods without the expense of building and staffing a new branch. For the church it's an unusual—but effective—way to generate income.

• **Telephone Service:** As if that's not enough, Global Telecom, Ventura, CA, offers a 900 number that channels money to the Pope. Consumers can dial 1 (900) 740-POPE to hear a prerecorded message (in English) by Pope John Paul II. The service costs $1.95 a minute, and approximately a third of the proceeds go to the Vatican.

How Long Should a CRM Campaign Last?

Pick the right answer:

1. As long as possible—to create the maximum opportunity for consumer response.
2. As short a time as possible—so it doesn't lose its appeal.

Actually, the real answer lies somewhere between those two extremes. Companies doing cause-related marketing walk a fine line between maximum exposure and consumer fatigue. To find a safe middle ground, successful campaigns tend to follow one of the following patterns:

- *Three-month campaigns:* The majority of cents-off coupon campaigns last three months. That's long enough to generate sufficient publicity, establish a strong presence in consumers' minds, and give them time to buy. It's short enough that the campaign doesn't lose its novelty. It also corresponds with a calendar quarter, making it easy to track results.
- *Three-week campaigns:* Many successful campaigns last only three weeks. These are frequently timed for the period between Thanksgiving and Christmas, when shoppers are being reminded to "remember the needy." Food manufacturers and retailers often carry out their campaigns at this time, with the contributions going to food banks and homeless shelters.
- *One-week campaigns:* One week is a short period in which to advertise a campaign and get consumers to act. But it's been known to work—and work well—when tied to a specific event. Ralston Purina, for example, has timed a CRM campaign with the National Humane Society to coincide with National Pet Week. Tying a campaign to a preexisting event is a good way to generate additional publicity.
- *Annual campaigns:* While most companies design CRM campaigns as single events, numerous companies have built their campaigns into annual promotions. They occur each year at the same time, frequently in coordination with a preexisting event. Thus each year's campaign reinforces previous campaigns in consumers' minds. For example, Procter & Gamble carries out a CRM campaign with the Special Olympics every year, raising millions of dollars for the cause. The repetition of the campaign cements the association between the company and the Special Olympics, producing residual benefit to the company even at other times of the year.

"Permanent" CRM

One of the more interesting twists on CRM was achieved by Scott Paper Company, which in 1986 created a line of products called Helping Hand. Each product package bore the message "Every time you buy Helping Hand, you help children with special needs'' and explained that a nickel from each purchase went into a fund for six charities fighting children's diseases. Scott was betting that the cause-related nature of the product would differentiate the line from look-alike paper products and spur sales on a permanent basis. Scott was right. Helping Hand sales were good: the line was profitable, although slightly less so than Scott's other lines because of the donation. But the profits generated were in addition to—rather than pirated from—Scott's other lines. From the charities' standpoint, the line was quite successful, generating close to $3 million in five years. The line also solidified Scott's image as a company that cares about families, its target market. However, in 1991 the line was discontinued ''due to constraints in manufacturing capacity.''

The Danger in Cause-Related Marketing

A word of warning.

The danger in cause-related marketing is that it looks so easy. So easy to look good. So easy to make money. So easy to get in and out fast. The trouble with that attitude is that it makes it so easy to fail. So easy for a campaign to backfire because it's perceived not as *helping* a nonprofit, but as *using* a nonprofit to sell a product. As more and more companies jump onto the CRM bandwagon, consumers are getting wiser. They can sniff out the frauds.

As we said before, you must be sincere. If you decide to pursue cause-related marketing, don't do it as a one-shot thing. Make it part of a continuing partnership with a nonprofit you care about. Use other elements to enhance your campaign—in-kind donations, employee volunteers, special events. These will further the cause and let the world know you're really committed. Consumers will support your campaign because they support your partner. They want to know you genuinely support your partner, too.

CHAPTER 7

Sponsorships

Blame it on inflated media costs. Blame it on ad clutter, ad nauseam. Blame it on turned-off, channel-surfing consumers, numbed by mass-market, vanilla-flavor advertising. Making an impact through traditional media has never been tougher. . . . Companies have never needed sponsorship more.

—Lesa Ukman, president, International Events Group
publisher, Special Events Report

Back in 1951, when Sam E. Miller, a Jamaica, New York, bartender, community gossip, and pop-fly hitter extraordinaire, decided to place the Blue Spot Tavern's distinctive baby-blue logo on the backs of the Steele Street Boys' softball team, it set him back a cool $127—and a couple of rounds of beer every Thursday night. Today's corporate sponsorships cost quite a bit more, and the drink of choice is more likely to be champagne than draft. But the reasons for trying them and the results they produce are exactly the same. A positive company image. Improved community relations. And, it's hoped, a little new business. What's new about sponsorships in the 1990s is the variety of events that are being planned—and the number of companies that are carrying them out.

Today corporate sponsorship is a $2.9-*billion*-a-year industry, with thousands of companies sponsoring sports races, art exhibits, symphony and rock concerts, walk-a-thons, bike-a-thons, and other events, mostly in partnership with nonprofit organizations. They run the gamut from low-budget local tie-ins like the Blue Spot Tavern's to multimillion-dollar extravaganzas broadcast over national TV. Perhaps more than any other form of partnership, event sponsorship holds something for everyone.

Why the rush to sponsor events? Sponsorships are particularly well suited to a variety of corporate goals.

- *Marketing* goals can be met by designing an event to appeal to a target market. Retailers can be brought in to stimulate sales and traffic at the retail level. Merchandising opportunities can be built in to sell event-related products which provide lasting in-home reminders.
- *Community affairs* goals can be met by designing an event that responds to needs in the community and by working with community liaisons in its implementation.
- *Employee relations* needs can be met by supplying a framework for employee participation. Events can build pride in and provide perks for your workers.
- *Philanthropic* goals can be met by picking an event that falls within your corporate giving policy.
- *Public relations* goals can be met by designing an event that is unusual and therefore of interest to the media.

On the nonprofit side, the benefits are equally substantial. Events offer nonprofits a great way to get their message out—through the event itself and through attendant publicity. They spur people to action on the nonprofit's behalf—by collecting pledges, by attending a concert, by cleaning up a lake. And they can collect money from the public for the organization—through donations or an admission fee.

Events can be remarkably flexible—tailored to the needs of the partners. They can be big one-time national celebrations, like the Statue of Liberty extravaganza on the Fourth of July 1984. They can be continuing national events that travel from city to city, being altered to fit each city along the way. Or they can be strictly local events that touch one city, or even one neighborhood. Special events can be tailored to an issue, to a geographic or socioeconomic market, and to a budget level.

The down side of events is that they can be logistically complicated. They require large numbers of bodies—paid or volunteer. They tend to have many details, which means lots of room for things to go wrong. They frequently depend on wholly undependable phenomena, like weather. And they require more of your time for organizing and orchestrating than some other forms of partnership. But if you have staff time and energy and a good nonprofit partner on whom you can depend for a lot of legwork, they can be well worth the hassles.

The following stories describe two event sponsorships. Both involve museums, but there the likeness ends. These particular events were chosen to show the range of sponsorship options available even with one type of nonprofit, and to show the ways sponsorship can be used to meet very different corporate needs.

Citibank and *Black Achievers in Science*

In 1986 Citibank's Chicago office asked the Museum of Science and Industry the kind of question museums love to hear: what kind of exhibition can we fund for $25,000 or $50,000? Citibank believed that such a sizable grant to a major cultural institution would strengthen the bank's Chicago presence. Citibank was more than a little surprised, however, when the museum came back with a proposal for a temporary exhibit on black achievements in science—with a price tag of $300,000. That was just a little out of the ballpark, and the Chicago office said no. Enter Betsy Howland, then Citibank's vice-president for contributions and community affairs. Although $300,000 for a local exhibition was out of the question, Howland saw the exhibit's potential as a national event and decided to go to bat for it.

Meeting Needs, Internally and Externally

Nationally, the exhibit's message pushed a lot of buttons. Just three years earlier, the seminal report *A Nation at Risk* had come out, criticizing America's public education system for failing to meet its students' needs. Ever since, the media were filled with debates about how to improve the nation's schools. Since minorities seemed to bear the brunt of the failing system, anything that promoted black role models was to be applauded.

Internally the exhibit pushed a lot of buttons, too. To understand just how many, you need to understand Citibank's structure. At that time, Citibank was decentralized into three divisions: individual banking, which served individual depositors and loan applicants; institutional banking, which served businesses and institutions; and investment banking, which served the needs of investors. Each division had its own marketing and philanthropic departments.

Howland's department was institutional (or "corporate") philanthropy. The exhibition met her needs because it tackled a pressing national problem in an innovative way. (Ever since the publication of *A Nation at Risk,* she had been urging the bank to beef up its efforts in precollegiate education.) It also helped that the executives of many of the bank's corporate customers sat on boards of museums around the country. They would be pleased to see the bank sponsor a national museum exhibition tour.

But Howland was shrewd enough to realize that the benefits from the exhibition would not end with her department. The exhibit would draw large minority and inner-city audiences, a target market for all banks, which, prevented from redlining by the Community Reinvestment Act, must show that they are meeting the needs of low- to moderate-income populations. This would appeal to the goals of the individual banking division. The exhibit would enable bank representatives to meet local officials in cities on the tour. This would meet the needs of the government relations department. The exhibit would showcase the type of activity the bank engenders in its branch cities. This would be helpful in opening new markets. All of the departments realized that a relationship with the prestigious and popular Museum of Science and Industry would strengthen the bank's reputation in one of its largest cities, and that a national tour would strengthen its image and presence around the country.

The exhibit provided something for almost everyone. And since, as Howland said, "any grant over $10,000 has to be justified left, right and center," that panoply of benefits was essential to getting the project funded. Using corporate philanthropic money, the bank underwrote the development and fabrication of the exhibit for $300,000. Later, money would come from other departments to create educational programs and materials, to hold parties, and to produce marketing materials. At one point someone asked Howland whether they wouldn't be better off spending the money on scholarships. She replied emphatically, "No. That way we reach just a small number of students. This way we inspire hundreds of thousands of students."

Once the museum began planning the exhibit, the bank stayed out of its way. Citibank's philosophy: *We give this institution money because we trust what they do. If we're asked for an opinion we'll give it, but we won't interfere.* The results were impressive: a 2,000-square-foot interactive exhibition featuring the achievements of sixteen distinguished black American scientists. It also gave practical information about how to prepare for a career in science. *Black Achievers* opened at the Museum of Science and Industry in February 1988, timed to coordinate with Black History Month. To maximize Citibank's presence, the bank's Chicago branches sponsored Black Creativity, the museum's annual Black History Month festival celebrating black culture. To promote the exhibit's opening, the bank hired a national black public relations firm, which proved exceptionally skilled at marketing to the black community. The firm targeted media people who were particularly receptive to the project; identified spokespeople for the exhibit, within Citibank and among the scientists featured in the show; and arranged for an opening gala and press releases, getting the story onto the Associated Press wire. The museum advertised the exhibition along downtown's Michigan Avenue on banners which bore the names of the exhibit and the museum, as well as the Citibank logo.

The Tour

As the museum planned the tour, Citibank negotiated with each host museum for the right of first refusal to sponsor local educational programs. It then told its local branches that it would supplement their funds with corporate money if they funded the museums' local programs. The resulting range of programs was quite large. It included college entrance exam preparation courses in Fort Worth for black students who showed promise in science; a Career Day in New York City featuring black scientists and professionals (Citibank had a booth at the fair to tell young people how to get a job at the bank); and a program in Chicago in which the museum sent the exhibition's black designer and some of the featured scientists into local high schools.

Promotion in each city was left to individual Citibank offices. To help them, the bank created a small brochure and poster which were available at the exhibit and at each Citibank branch. In keeping with company philosophy, these pieces bore a one-sentence credit line and a small Citibank logo as the only bank identification. The company believes that a fine line exists between sponsor "identification" and "commercialization," and prefers to keep its identification tasteful and uncompromising. Paid advertising was used only in New York City. Although additional advertising would have been nice, the bank thought it was too expensive, and that the same money would be better spent on educational programs which would promote the exhibit in a "softer" way and create positive word-of-mouth exposure.

Citibank also paid for the creation of a Teachers' Guide, which Howland quickly realized had potential to stand alone as an educational piece for people who never saw the exhibit. To maximize its use, they printed an additional 100,000 copies, which they distributed to educational and civic groups around the country.

The exhibit was originally scheduled to visit eight cities, of which most, but not all, had a significant Citibank presence. As it turned out, additional cities, including New York and Washington, D.C., were added along the way. The visit to Washington was added to coincide with both the Black Caucus, an annual convention attended by blacks in government affairs, and the opening of Citibank's new government relations office. Citibank hosted an opening reception, attended by then mayor Marion Barry, which enabled the bank to showcase its new office as well as its commitment to black concerns. The New York opening, with a surprise visit by New York mayor David Dinkins, gave the exhibition a particularly strong presence in the company's headquarters city.

Results

In all, *Black Achievers in Science* visited twelve cities and was seen by approximately five and a half million people. Citibank's initial commitment of $300,000 grew to approximately $750,000 as the bank willingly added local educational and promotional elements. Was the expense worth it? Citibank believes it was. The variety of benefits— to the bank and to the host communities—would have been difficult to achieve in any other way. The bank reached millions of people in its target audience with a powerful and positive message, and it made valuable contacts in the cities to which the exhibit traveled. Local museums attracted record numbers of black visitors, beginning a dialogue with a generally underserved audience. And museum visitors learned about black role models, and saw that a path exists from innercity schools to success.

As a result of the exhibit, Citibank has created a continuing partnership with the Museum of Science and Industry. Local Citibank branches have sponsored the Black Creativity program every year since 1988, and the Bank has agreed to refurbish the exhibit and fund its return visit to the Museum of Science and Industry and a second national tour.

Did the exhibit make a difference in people's lives? That kind of thing is hard to measure. But one girl's story suggests that it helped some visitors see new possibilities for their lives. A black inner-city high school senior after being bused to the exhibit decided to go on to college and to major in pre-med.

Coldwell Banker and the Toy Fair

At the opposite end of the event sponsorship spectrum is the Coldwell Banker Toy Fair. Whereas the Citibank exhibit was national, the Toy Fair was local. Whereas the Citibank event lasted several years, the Toy Fair took place over a weekend. Whereas Citibank drew hundreds of thousands of dollars from many budgets and met many corporate needs, the Toy Fair cost $15,000 and met two specific marketing goals. Did we say event sponsorship is a flexible option?

Coldwell Banker is a franchised real estate chain with offices nationwide. By and large, individual offices do their own marketing in response to local needs. The Denver office had two very specific needs. It wanted to boost its name recognition with local families, and it wanted to build traffic into its offices. How to accomplish those things—creatively and inexpensively? The question was answered when the Denver Children's Museum called with an offer.

The museum in those days was constantly developing ideas for products, services, and events we could do in partnership with corporations to get our educational messages out to families and to generate income. In a 1982 brainstorm session we had come up with the idea of developing a holiday toy swap for families which would also provide toys for kids in orphanages and hospitals. What company would want to sponsor an event like that? How about a real estate company that wants to reach families? Playing a hunch, we called Coldwell Banker. The company liked the idea and we struck a deal.

The Children's Museum was the primary event planner. We decided to hold the event in a hotel ballroom—big enough to hold large crowds, central enough to draw people from the whole Denver metropolitan area. It would take place over a weekend in early December to capitalize on the holiday gift-giving spirit and to get gifts to institutionalized kids in time for Christmas. Families would be invited to come to the event bringing three old toys in good condition. One toy would be set aside for charity. The other two would be placed on giant tables, sorted by category—games, stuffed animals, dolls, and so on.

Once families had delivered their two old toys, they would be free to browse among the toys other families had brought and pick two to take home. The fair would be supervised by museum staff and volunteers and by Coldwell Banker brokers. This gave the brokers a chance to participate in a fun event—and to meet prospective clients face to face.

To draw attention to the event and to Coldwell Banker's participation, the company agreed to do all the advertising. They bought print and radio ads and included information about the event in mailings to all their former and prospective customers. We advertised the fair in our members' newsletter and placed public service announcements with local radio stations. Coldwell Banker also produced banners bearing the fair's name and the company and museum logos and hung them in its local branches and at the hotel. At Coldwell Banker's request, we included an element designed specifically to build traffic into the company's offices. For three weeks before the fair, families could go to Coldwell Banker to get free tickets and to drop off toys in advance. This meant that even people who couldn't attend the fair still had a way of participating. It also drew the attention of thousands of families who were delighted to suddenly have a guilt-free way to clear their closets. Thousands of parents located their nearest Coldwell Banker office, used it to make a tax-deductible donation, left their names and addresses behind, and walked away with Coldwell Banker literature. It was probably one of the more benevolent prospecting tools ever designed.

The price tag for this event? Coldwell Banker paid the museum $15,000 from its contributions budget. It supplemented this with advertising money to create the ads and banners. What did the realtor get in exchange? The company didn't quantify the results, but the take seemed pretty clear: a lot of goodwill; a lot of attention from its target audience; and thousands of names of potential customers.

Event Sponsorships and the IRS

Event sponsorships are such good marketing vehicles for corporations that recently the IRS has begun to notice. In late 1991, the agency challenged two nonprofits' claims that sponsorship fees paid by corporate sponsors were donations, ruling that they were actually advertising fees, for which the companies received substantial advertising benefits. Now, before you get nervous and decide that sponsorships are something to avoid, let us reassure you. This ruling should have no impact on your decision to sponsor a nonprofit event. For one thing, the two events involved were college bowl games—very big, very visible multimillion-dollar sponsorships. The IRS is not interested in investigating small events, or even many other large events. And corporations are not directly affected by the ruling, which merely requires that these two nonprofit organizations pay income tax on their sponsorship fees. Their sponsors' taxes are not affected. The only impact on corporations will come if nonprofits raise their sponsorship fees in the future to cover an anticipated tax bite. Moreover, if an event is designed to promote a nonprofit's mission, income it receives in support should be related to the group's mission, and therefore tax-exempt. You can read more about event sponsorship and nonprofit tax issues in Chapter 29, ''Nonprofits and Legal Issues.'' For now, suffice it to say that sponsorships are a safe and mutually beneficial form of partnership. Concern about nonprofit taxes should not scare you away.

CHAPTER 8

Premiums

The development of partnerships between corporations and nonprofits has put a whole new spin on the premium market. Finally there's an alternative to giving customers that same old logo-bearing coffee mug. Or calendar. Or appointment book. These days you can give them a customized product that truly reflects your business, that genuinely meets their need, and that comes with the credibility of a well-respected nonprofit. Is your market families? How about giving them a four-color book of games for the whole family, produced by a recognized expert in family education, the local children's museum? Or perhaps a kit of security tips for home and office produced by the nation's experts in crime prevention, the National Crime Prevention Council? Once you start doing your premium shopping at nonprofit agencies, you've got a wide-open field for finding a truly unique product—at a very reasonable price.

The Denver Children's Museum may be the nonprofit leader in developing corporate premium items. Between 1977 and 1984 we sold close to twenty products to corporations, which they used for a variety of purposes.

StarKist/9-Lives: Reaching a Target Market

Kids and Pets was our premium item for StarKist/9-Lives. In 1981 StarKist wanted to boost sales of 9-Lives cat food. It also wanted to beef up its relationship with veterinarians. So the corporation hired the Denver Children's Museum to produce an educational booklet about pets which was aimed at kids and families. Of course, the company knew from seeing other Children's Museum publications that the book wouldn't be dull and boring, but would be a high-quality, illustration-packed activity book that families would use and keep. We customized the book by putting the 9-Lives trademark, Sylvester the Cat, on the cover and a message from the CEO inside. StarKist bought 62,000 copies at $1.25 each. It gave 12,000 to veterinarians. The other 50,000 it used as a self-liquidating premium for the twenty-pound bag of 9-Lives. When the deal was done, the museum had made a profit and had spread its name and message across the country. StarKist had made it into veterinarians' offices *and* built its loyalty with families, who saw the company as responsive to their needs.

Citicorp: Building Business

The museum also produced a dual-purpose premium book for Citicorp—although the second purpose didn't emerge until after the fact. Citicorp came to the museum in 1983 because it wanted to attract customers to its Person to Person Financial Centers. The bank's target market was middle-income families—a group the museum knew well. To help the bank attract them, we produced *Small Change,* a thirty-two–page book for kids on money and the economy. Citicorp bought 60,000 copies and gave one to every new loan customer. When a Citicorp banker took the book into his son's fifth-grade class one day and it got a rave review, a second use unexpectedly appeared. Citicorp purchased 250,000 additional copies to give to upper-elementary classrooms in communities where it was building business. The bank knew the books would eventually reach parents—exactly the market they were courting.

Citicorp: Strengthening Customer Relationships

In perhaps one of the more unusual twists on the use of premium items, Citicorp actually hired the entire New York Philharmonic as a thank-you present for its preferred European business customers. The financial services company hired the orchestra for a private series of European concerts. The concerts provided a lovely evening for Citicorp clients; they also reinforced Citicorp's image of quality. The Philharmonic benefited as well, earning additional revenue from the tour and meeting new audiences and new potential funders.

Children's World: Encouraging Repeat Business

Children's World, owner of day-care centers across the country, also found an unusual, but effective, way to buy premium items, again from the Children's Museum. In 1982 and '83 instead of hiring us to produce a product for them, they merely bought bulk museum memberships at a discount and gave them as premiums to families who reenrolled their children for a second year. Through the program, the museum reached many more families with its message and memberships—and Children's World bought a lot of repeat business.

Levi Strauss & Co.: Building Retail Activity

Levi's used a premium produced by the Bank Street College of Education in a marketing program involving its retailers. Hoping to attract more buyers to its line of children's clothing, in 1986 the company sought the help of Bank Street, a nonprofit leader in child development and education, located in New York City. Bank Street devised a three-part program focusing on the hassles—and educational potential—of dressing a preschooler. The college created a short in-store video (formated as a kids' version of the evening news), a thirty-two-page activity book for children (featuring Levi's characters Buttons the Pup and Rivets the Frog), and a thirteen-page booklet for parents called *Dressing Your Preschooler with Less Hassle.* The three pieces were given to Levi's retailers just before the holiday shopping season for in-store promotional displays and giveaways. Levi's purposely kept the company presence in the three pieces to a minimum to maximize the pieces' educational credibility. A brief message to parents from the CEO appeared on the activity book's back cover, explaining Levi's interest in providing the highest-quality children's clothing as well as educational information important to its customers. By partnering one of the highest-quality forces in children's education, Levi's reinforced those messages to its customers.

Ballard Realty: Attracting Attention

William Shakespeare: the greatest apartment salesman of our time. That's not how most of us think of the Bard, but that's what he proved to be for Ballard Realty of Montgomery, Alabama. Ballard offered a subscription to the Alabama Shakespeare Festival to each person who signed a lease at its new Stratford Village Apartments, and, as a result, leased 80 percent of the units before construction was completed. Ballard filled the remaining 20 percent shortly after by using lines from Shakespeare to highlight amenities in the apartments. The festival benefited, too—from the publicity generated by the unusual ad campaign and from the new audience members the company recruited. The success of this program led the Business Committee for the Arts, Inc., a national organization of business leaders committed to advocating business support of the arts, to feature this partnership in its national advertising campaign.

Texize: Using Premiums as Part of a Multilayered Public Purpose Campaign

The Texize Division of Dow Consumer Products (now Dow Brands in Indianapolis), manufacturer of (among other things) home cleaning products, also teamed up with the National Crime Prevention Council (NCPC) to develop premium items. But then Texize tossed in a cause-related marketing campaign *and* a strategy to benefit local retailers.

NCPC had developed a McGruff Drug Prevention and Personal Protection curriculum for elementary-school students. The curriculum used NCPC's well-known crime dog, McGruff, to teach kids how to protect themselves from crime. In a national media campaign, Texize advertised that for every 200 cases of its products ordered by a store, the company would donate a one-grade McGruff curriculum package to a school of the retailer's choice. For every 1,000 cases bought, Texize would donate a curriculum package for the entire school.

Texize also made a shortened version of the curriculum available to parents as a self-liquidating premium. The company purchased McGruff hand puppets and audiotapes from NCPC and offered them to parents for $4.99 and one proof-of-purchase seal from any Texize product. Simultaneously, the company ran a conventional CRM coupon campaign in which they donated $.20 to NCPC for every coupon redeemed.

The results of the tripartite campaign were staggering. NCPC

The greatest apartment salesman of our time

To most of us, William Shakespeare is the quintessential playwright.

But when the Ballard Realty Company of Montgomery, Alabama, needed tenants for a new apartment complex, Mr. Shakespeare proved to be a top-notch salesman as well. With every signed lease, Ballard Realty offered free membership subscriptions to the nearby Alabama Shakespeare Festival. In no time, over 80% of the company's units were leased before construction was even completed.

Throughout the country, small and medium-sized businesses, like Ballard Realty, are discovering what blue chippers have known for years: that the arts can help create a positive public image, increase a company's visibility and improve sales. All this while reducing taxable income.

If you would like information on how your company—no matter what its size—can benefit through a partnership with the arts, contact the Business Committee for the Arts, Inc., 1775 Broadway, Suite 510, New York, New York 10019, or call (212) 664-0600.

It may just be the factor that decides whether this year's sales goals are to be or not to be.

BUSINESS COMMITTEE FOR THE ARTS, INC.

This advertisement prepared as a public service by Ogilvy & Mather.

received more than $200,000 in donations and reached millions of children and families with its crime prevention message. Texize experienced its best quarter ever.

The Power of Premiums,
Nonprofit-Style

Purchasing premium items from nonprofits has clear benefits for corporations:

- It gives your company a unique product, strongly differentiated from the competition's.
- It gives you a product tailored to your needs, rather than a generic product off a supply-house shelf.
- It gives you a product that meets the needs of your target market and is therefore an effective business-building tool.
- It gives you a product that is credible, creative, and associated with a worthy cause, strengthening your corporation's image.

The strategy has equally clear benefits for nonprofits:

- It enables them to reach a much larger audience with their message than they would ever reach on their own.
- It provides unrestricted operating cash.
- It pays them to do what they do best: create educational products that carry out their mission.

CHAPTER 9

Licensing

At the end of the day it's the power of the panda that counts. The World Wildlife Fund's famous symbol . . . has been used to do everything from creating awareness and building brand loyalty to encouraging trial and increasing sales.

—*Business Sponsorship of the Environment,*
a publication of the World Wildlife Fund

In 1985 you didn't need to hear it through the grapevine to know that the hottest vocal group around was a bunch of overweight lunchbox-toting construction workers called the California Raisins. Within weeks of their first hit commercial, their wrinkled bodies were appearing on plush toys, radios, clothing, and a host of other consumer products. What many people didn't realize was that the four crooners and all the products they adorned were licensed products of the California Raisin Board, and that in addition to touting the goodness of raisins, they were raisin' lots of dough for the nonprofit Raisin Board and its corporate partners.

Licensing partnerships between nonprofits and corporations are hardly new. Universities have long licensed manufacturers of pennants, jackets, book covers, mugs, and other paraphernalia to produce products bearing the university insignia. Large associations such as trade unions and professional groups have also licensed the manufacturing of products, primarily for their members. However, over the last decade the number of licensing deals has grown as both corporations and nonprofits have recognized the income-generating potential of nonprofit names, logos, and properties.

A licensing agreement is a relatively simple way of purchasing the nonprofit's name or logo to place on your product. The nonprofit, as owner of the logo, is the licensor. You are the licensee. In exchange for the use of the logo on a designated product for a designated period, you pay the nonprofit a royalty, a percentage of the price of every product sold. Most companies use licensing agents to find partners and work out the details of the agreement, although some larger companies that do a great deal of licensing handle it internally.

Companies have used licensing arrangements with nonprofits to meet a variety of needs.

Expanding a Product Line

Licensing a product from a nonprofit can add a level of cachet to your product line that would be unavailable with a corporate licensor, since the product comes complete with the image and appeal of the nonprofit. For example, when Spring Industries, Inc., in New York wanted to create a tony new line of bed linens, it went to the Metropolitan Museum of Art and licensed the rights to textile designs in the collection. The result: an upscale line of "classic" bedsheets.

Attracting a Target Market

Licensing a product from a nonprofit enables you to attract that organization's market. The best example is the ubiquitous *Sesame Street* characters. If you've ever wandered the aisles of Toys "R"

Us, you know you can't go far without running into Big Bird, Ernie, and the rest of the gang from the popular television show. Lunch-boxes, clothing, dolls, school supplies, room decorations . . . the list goes on and on. Each of those images has been licensed from Children's Television Workshop, the nonprofit organization that produces the show. And each has turned an otherwise undistinguished item into a must-have for millions of *Sesame Street* fans.

Building Credibility

Recognizing the interest boys have in space and science, Toys "R" Us wanted to offer a line of space toys. Where to get good-quality toys that would be well received? Toys "R" Us teamed up with the Young Astronauts Council, a nonprofit organization whose mission is to promote interest in space and science among children. Young Astronauts developed a line of twenty-four space-related educational toys and licensed Toys "R" Us to sell them. The agreement produced continuing income and exposure for the nonprofit, and helped millions of youngsters have fun while learning about science. Toys "R" Us got a distinctive line of products that met a perceived need.

Repositioning a Product

Tying a product to a nonprofit through licensing can be an effective way to reposition an otherwise undistinguished performer, by giving it an identity that makes it stand out from the crowd. For example, Cadbury, the British chocolate maker, wanted to increase the sales of its twenty-gram chocolate bar. Market research had shown that the target market liked animals and was interested in animal causes. So Cadbury approached the World Wildlife Fund. In a licensing agreement with the fund, Cadbury repositioned the bar as the Cadbury Wildlife

Bar, placing the WWF logo on the wrapper and paying a royalty to the organization for every bar sold. Sales increased by 35 percent in the first year.

Licensing on a Local Level

Licensing can also be done on a local level to build an association between a product or company and a local nonprofit with a devoted following. Meadow Gold Dairies in Denver wanted to bring out a new fruit drink aimed at children. To give the drink a distinctive personality, the company teamed up with the Denver Children's Museum, licensing the museum's mascot, a fuzzy creature named the Nuzz. The company named the drink Nuzz Juice, and placed the Nuzz image and the museum's logo on each carton. The arrangement gave the museum a respectable income stream and gave the company a product that stood out from the crowd.

Licensing for a Short-Term Association with a Nonprofit

Licensing agreements are generally used to give a corporation long-term use of a nonprofit's logo. However, it is also possible to license a nonprofit's logo for a short-term event. Suppose, for instance, you wanted to sponsor the local symphony orchestra to create a summer concert series in a park. You could give the orchestra a charitable donation to cover its time. Then, to advertise the concerts, you might license the right to put the orchestra's logo in your ads and on signs and banners bearing your name.

A simpler way to achieve the same result would be to pay the orchestra a sponsorship fee which would cover both its time and the right to use its logo. However, more companies may choose the licensing route in the future because of the recent IRS ruling regarding sponsorship fees, mentioned earlier.

How Nonprofits See Licensing Agreements

Of all the forms of partnership, licensing is the one that nonprofits have been the slowest to embrace. A licensing agent we spoke to recently, who works exclusively with corporate clients, said, "I tried working with nonprofits a few years ago. I had to give it up. It was too frustrating. *Did* they want to do it? *Didn't* they want to do it? They couldn't decide." It's true; nonprofits have mixed responses to licensing. On the one hand, they want to do it because they want the benefits it can bring in terms of money and exposure. On the other hand, several factors argue against it.

One is the nonprofit's ever-vigilant concern with integrity. If a nonprofit sells its name and logo to a corporation, will it be perceived as too commercial? Will it tarnish its image as a trustworthy doer of good deeds? This concern is real and must be addressed by anyone who wants to license a nonprofit trademark. The way to address it is to license a nonprofit's name only for a product that genuinely promotes its mission.

A second concern is image. How will the nonprofit's name be used? Will it have any control? Will the product reflect the quality of the organization? These concerns are no different from those of a corporate licensor. Any product bearing an organization's name reflects that organization's image, so it had better be good. Address that concern the same way you would with a corporate partner. Assure the nonprofit that the product will be first-class and follow through. You want no less for your company.

A third reason that nonprofits are wary of licensing is concern about their time and energy. They fear that engaging in licensing will divert them from their primary purpose. With small staffs already stretched thin, they believe their goals are better met by pursuing their traditional programs. You can address this concern by helping your potential partner analyze the pros and cons of the program. How much time will it take to administer? Will the nonprofit need to add a staff person? Will the royalties it collects more than cover its time and expense? Is the return large enough to warrant the hassle? Performing a program analysis together can be a useful educational process for both partners and can help you build a good working relationship.

A fourth reason that some nonprofits are slow to embrace licensing has to do with the nonprofit culture, which does not lend itself to seeking—or seeing—licensing opportunities in its midst. Staff members focus on carrying out their mission, not on making money from it. As a result, licensing is a concept most nonprofits have simply never considered, and your prospective nonprofit partner may need some wooing. You may need to gradually cultivate the nonprofit's interest in the program, meeting with key executives and board members several times to educate them about the benefits licensing can bring.

It may help them to know that the nonprofits that have entered into licensing agreements have been extremely pleased with the results. They've found the increased exposure and the increased cash flow well worth the time spent developing and managing the program. It is entirely likely that as nonprofit enterprise grows in popularity, more and more organizations will discover the benefits of licensing and become eager to take part.

Licensing Rules of Thumb

If you decide to pursue licensing with a nonprofit partner, keep the following guidelines in mind:

- Make sure there is a logical relationship between the non-profit and the product: don't force a connection just to get an appealing name on your product. The public won't buy it. Sales will suffer. So may the reputation of the nonprofit.

• Make sure the product needs to exist: don't create a product just for the sake of putting a nonprofit's name on it. If the market doesn't need and want it, even the best name won't make it sell.

• Make sure the corporation and the nonprofit agree on the terms of the deal and the product before you begin. Differences are easier to iron out before production than after.

CHAPTER 10

Sponsored Advertisements

Help Smirnoff end illiteracy in America.

—Smirnoff Vodka ad to benefit Literacy
Volunteers of America, 1989

Corporations have long sponsored symphony concerts, art exhibitions, and special events with nonprofits. But in the last few years a new item has appeared on the sponsorship menu—one that may be simpler, less expensive, and equally effective. It is sponsored advertising, a program in which a corporation buys advertising for a nonprofit and includes its own message in the ad.

Nonprofits have traditionally relied on public service announcements to get their messages out. These free ads have been useful—they provide $3 billion of donated air time for nonprofits each year. But they have serious limitations. They tend to run at odd hours—never in prime time. There is no way to target them to specific audiences. They are harder and harder to get as more nonprofits compete for the limited slots. And they are extremely expensive to produce, averaging $150,000—well beyond the budget of all but the largest nonprofits. As a result, many groups have eagerly embraced the concept of sponsored ads.

Corporations, too, have warmed to the concept. Sponsored ads provide all the benefits of any other form of nonprofit partnership. They establish or reinforce a company's connection with a worthy cause. They can enhance a product's credibility. They can distinguish a product from its competition and expose a company to new markets.

For all these reasons, the number of sponsored ad campaigns is growing, with more corporations and more nonprofits getting in on the act. In some cases, nonprofits are approaching corporations with ideas for ads which the two organizations then produce together. In others, charities have sold corporations ads that are already produced, to which the corporation adds its own brief message. Other campaigns have been initiated by corporations, which add a brief nonprofit message to their own product or image pitch.

Sponsoring Ads to Strengthen Your Image: Bankers Trust

Bankers Trust in New York City takes its relationship with community groups seriously. Each year it gives hundreds of thousands of dollars to neighborhood organizations. That's not surprising; the health of the bank's neighborhoods has a direct bearing on the health of the bank. And besides, generating goodwill with neighbors never hurt business. But in 1989, the bank did something unusual. It gave $500,000 to community groups around the city, and then went one step further. With the help of its advertising agency, Doremus & Company, the bank picked five community groups to receive special attention. All five were doing the undoable—reinvigorating some of New York's worst neighborhoods through grass-roots community development projects.

The projects were so novel and so inspiring that Bankers Trust wanted people to know about them. The bank believed that publicizing the projects would further its goals by attracting people to the newly revitalized neighborhoods and by attracting money from other funders. So for each group, the bank created an elegant full-page ad highlighting the group's work and defying people's stereotype of the neighborhood. "A Bronx you can get lost in," said one, followed by lively copy about the Port Morris Antique Center, an oasis of "antiques, industry and optimism" created by the South Bronx Overall Economic Development Corporation. "An East New York you don't see on the nightly news," proclaimed another ad. Copy below extolled the work of homesteaders in Brooklyn, renewing their neighborhood with sweat equity. A third asserted, "It's not the Jamaica you change trains in," referring to a popular subway junction. The copy described a big farmers' market in Queens.

Surrounding the copy in each ad were striking black and white woodcut-style scenes from the neighborhoods: a man caning a chair and a couple carrying an antique vase in the Bronx ad; homesteaders sawing and painting their houses in the Brooklyn ad; fruit-and-vegetable vendors in the Queens ad. Below the artwork appeared two lines: "Born Again Neighborhoods. Bankers Trust is Proud to Help."

The ads ran in *The New York Times* at a cost of $25,000 apiece. To Bankers Trust that money was well spent. Not only did the campaign help five remarkable organizations, it helped Bankers Trust by solidifying its image as a bank that cares about its neighbors.

Small-Scale Sponsoring: Mataam Fez

Of course, sponsored ads also work on a much smaller scale. Years ago, at the Denver Children's Museum, one of our board members who owned a restaurant called Mataam Fez regularly tagged a line or two about the museum onto his print and radio ads. It didn't hurt his business to let customers know he was associated with the museum. And for the museum, it was a free and effective way to get the word out to hundreds of thousands of people about new exhibits and programs.

Used with permission of Bankers Trust Company.

Sponsoring Ads to Link Your Company to a Cause: Marion Merrell Dow

Bankers Trust used sponsored ads to tout the work of its grantees and its community service. Some companies have used the strategy with more of an eye on the bottom line.

Marion Merrell Dow, manufacturer of Nicorette, a nicotine gum prescribed by doctors to help patients stop smoking, has sponsored ads for the American Lung Association. The $3-million print and TV campaign advertised the association's annual "Non-Dependence Day" for smokers. Although the ads did not mention Nicorette by name, they did mention the name of the company. Apparently that association was enough: Marion continued the campaign for several years.

Although sponsored ads have been a blessing for many companies and nonprofits, some groups see them as a curse. Two concerns lead them to see the strategy as dangerous rather than beneficial. One is concern that by linking their message with a corporate pitch, nonprofits are implicitly endorsing products. The second is the fear that the rise of sponsored ads will reduce the availability of public service announcements.

Implied Endorsements

In the late 1980s Bristol-Myers Squibb ran a series of cable TV commercials in partnership with the American Heart Association (AHA). The sixty-second ads highlighted risk factors for heart disease and stroke. In the last fifteen seconds, Bristol-Myers advertised its painkiller, Bufferin. While the company was very pleased with the association between Bufferin and the AHA, the Heart Association was less enthusiastic. Its managers believed that the ads implied an endorsement of Bufferin as an antidote to heart disease. Shortly after, the AHA discontinued the use of sponsored ads, and now uses only public service announcements for media outreach.

Does this mean that sponsored ads must avoid mentioning product names? Not necessarily. This is a negotiated business. There are no hard-and-fast rules. The only rules are those made up by you and your partner. You need to know going into a partnership what your partner's concerns will be, and you need to be willing to work together to develop a campaign that is mutually satisfactory. Your partner will be concerned about implied endorsements because it wants to protect its integrity. That should be your concern, too. After all, that's why you're partnering a nonprofit instead of another company.

Death Knell to Public Service Announcements?

A second criticism that has been lobbed at sponsored ads is that they threaten the existence of PSA's. The fear: if the media can get paid to run nonprofit ads, will they continue to run PSA's for free? So far there is no indication that they won't. Major media outlets have not reduced the number of PSA slots available, and most media experts believe that the two advertising techniques *can* coexist—as long as nonprofits don't ask for both free and paid space at the same time.

In any event, sponsored ads seem to be here to stay. Corporations like their effectiveness. Most nonprofits like their reach. As long as consumers place a high value on helping social causes, sponsored ads are likely to remain a strong weapon in a company's marketing arsenal.

Going Too Far?

One form of sponsored advertising makes even some corporate marketers wince. The British Boy Scouts have introduced a program in which a corporation can buy the right to place its name and logo on a merit badge for three years. The cost of the sponsorship varies with the badge's popularity. The athletic badge (bought by Pentland Industries) costs about £45,000 ($78,000). Other badges sell for between £5,000 and £50,000; Meccano, a French toy manufacturer, has bought the craftsman badge, and Asda, a big retail chain, has bought the naturalist badge. As of late 1991, twelve out of eighty badges had been purchased—and a hundred thousand Boy Scouts were wearing logos on their chests.

But there's no fear—or hope—that this sponsorship opportunity will spread to the United States. The Boy Scouts of America have drawn up detailed guidelines concerning what type of commercial sponsorship is appropriate for their organization. *Not* appropriate, they say, is the use of uniformed Scouts to advertise a commercial product.

CHAPTER 11

Vendor Relationships

This flavor combines our super creamy vanilla ice cream with chunks of Rainforest Crunch, a new cashew and brazilian nut butter crunch. Money from the purchase of these nuts will help Brazilian forest peoples start a nut shelling cooperative that they'll own and operate. Rainforest Crunch helps to show that the rainforests are more profitable when their nuts, fruits and medicinal plants are cultivated for traditional harvest than when their trees are cut for short-term gain.

—message on Ben & Jerry's Rainforest Crunch ice cream carton

If you're an ice cream maven, you've probably read this message at least once by the light of the freezer. If so, the notion of buying products to benefit a cause will be familiar to you. If not, the idea may seem a bit unorthodox. But in fact, many companies buy products to benefit causes because they know that by buying from nonprofits they benefit themselves as well.

What could you possibly buy from a nonprofit? And why would you want to buy from one of them when you can get what you need from for-profit suppliers?

Just like for-profit businesses, nonprofits sell their expertise. Dance companies sell performances (and sometimes classes). Counseling centers sell therapy. Environmental organizations sell information and services to protect the environment. Economic development groups sell services to rebuild inner cities. Job training centers sell the labor of their trainees. The range of products and services is as large as the number of fields in which nonprofits operate—which is to say it is virtually limitless. Chances are, many of the products and services you now purchase from for-profit suppliers could also be purchased from nonprofit organizations.

Now, we're not recommending that you switch all, or even most, of your vendor business to nonprofit suppliers. We're merely saying that doing business with a nonprofit is possible. It is also, sometimes, beneficial, because buying from a nonprofit can provide many of the same benefits that come with other forms of public purpose partnership. For instance:

- Unlike goods from a for-profit supplier, a nonprofit's offerings come factory-loaded with goodwill, which rubs off on your business.
- Nonprofits are experts in their fields. In fact, they are often the most qualified source of information or expertise in their area. So if you are looking for an authority in a particular field, a nonprofit may be your best resource.
- Nonprofits pack credibility. If you want to offer—to the public or to your employees—a product or service that inspires confidence, a nonprofit may be your best supplier.
- Nonprofits can offer access to new markets. If you want to reach a target market, purchasing a product or service from a nonprofit that attracts that audience can help you do so.
- Nonprofits can tailor products and services to your needs. Unlike a commercial supplier, which supplies the same product or service to multiple clients, a nonprofit is likely to develop a unique relationship with you, designing a customized product or service to meet your needs and its own.
- And, of course, nonprofits need the income and exposure that can come from selling their products and services to corpo-

rations. If you buy a product or service from a nonprofit, you know that you are helping it achieve its mission.

Vendor relationships with nonprofits run the gamut from very sophisticated to very simple. They can be long-term arrangements or very short-term contracts. The following examples will give you an idea of the range of products and services nonprofits provide and the range of corporate needs they are hired to meet.

Expanding a Product Line

The Bureau of Business Practice (BBP) is a division of publisher Simon & Schuster. Specializing in products for the business market, BBP publishes books, workbooks, videotapes, and other products that help businesses strengthen their management practices. In the late 1980s, BBP realized that cigarette smoking had become an issue in the workplace. As information grew about the dangers of sidestream smoke, nonsmokers were beginning to ask their employers to provide smoke-free work spaces. Companies were asking for products to help them develop smoking guidelines. BBP decided to add such a product. Who could produce it? BBP hired the Seattle, Washington, Smoking Policy Institute, a small nonprofit whose mission was to educate the public about the dangers of sidestream smoke and to help organizations develop smoking policies. Not only was the institute a respected expert in the field, but it came with the endorsement of the U.S. surgeon general. BBP paid the institute to create a videotape and workbook explaining how to design and implement a smoking policy, and bought the exclusive distribution rights. The institute now receives a royalty from every sale of the package, and its message is distributed to more companies than it could reach on its own. BBP acquired a new product from the leading expert in the field and added the credibility of the nonprofit institute to its product line.

Providing a Needed Service

The Hidden Valley Corporation (this company preferred not to have its real name used) owned a 6,500-acre parcel of land on the edge of a large Southern city. The corporation wanted to develop the land, but was aware that residents of the city valued the property as open space. How could the corporation maximize its opportunity for revenue generation while appeasing local citizens? In 1991 Hidden Valley hired the Conservation Fund, a nonprofit organization whose mission is to conduct real estate transactions that promote conservation of open space and historic and natural resources. The fund helped the corporation work out a plan for the property that included the development of a mixed-use community, an open space park and trail system, and buffer areas between the two. Fund staff also worked with the company's developer, architect, and engineers to assure that the appearance of the development reflected the beauty of the natural surroundings. As a result of the partnership, the fund achieved its goal of preserving a portion of the land as open space. Hidden Valley established itself as a leader in planned developments by creating a model that will likely be replicated across the nation.

Helping Gain Access to New Markets

Besides its health products business, Johnson & Johnson develops and implements corporate wellness programs. It markets the programs primarily to *Fortune* 500 companies, which use them to encourage healthy life-styles among their employees. In marketing the programs to companies, J&J wants to reach the senior individual involved with employee health and safety. How to find that person? How to get him or her to notice? As did BBP, Johnson & Johnson worked with the Smoking Policy Institute. The institute had produced a videotape designed to introduce companies to the issue of workplace smoking, and was now looking for a way to distribute the tape to corporations. In 1987 Johnson & Johnson gave the nonprofit a grant to pay for mailing the video to fifty *Fortune* 500 companies. The company bargained that the videotape, which was accompanied by a letter from the surgeon general, would find its way into the hands of the senior person responsible for employee health. That's exactly what happened. The company developed several contacts as a result of the mailing, meeting its own goal of market research at the same time that it helped the institute broadcast its message.

Adding Value to a Program or Product

Of course Johnson & Johnson was right: thousands of companies do want to provide wellness programs to their employees, and most don't want to develop the programs in-house. Some companies buy their wellness programs "off the shelf" from other companies, such as Johnson & Johnson. But some companies prefer to develop some components themselves and then supplement those with add-ons. Where to go for credible health promotion materials? Thousands of companies go to the nonprofit Hope Heart Institute in Seattle, a leading cardiovascular research facility, headed by Dr. Lester Sauvage, who performed the world's first open-heart surgery there in 1962. Besides conducting research and training doctors in cardiovascular medicine, the institute produces educational materials about cardiovascular health. Recognizing the need of corporations for wellness materials, the institute began publishing a monthly newsletter, the *Hope Heart Letter,* containing easy-to-read articles on nutrition, exercise, medical cost containment, stress reduction, and other "lifestyle" topics. Today thousands of companies purchase the newsletter, customize it with their own name and information, and distribute it to their employees. They hope the articles will help employees remain healthy—and help keep their health benefit costs down.

Meeting Employee Needs

The nonprofit agency Impact House, in Pasadena, California, has long offered counseling and treatment for people with alcohol and drug problems. Because the agency's government contracts did not cover the full cost of treatment, the organization began offering its services to corporations. Lockheed, Xerox, Pacific Bell, and other major employers have contracted with Impact House to provide counseling services to their employees. The contracts provide stable income to the agency and a valuable service to the corporations.

Meeting an Internal Need

The Minneapolis warehouse of Target Stores receives hundreds of "vendor samples" every week. These are items that the store is considering carrying. Once the items have been examined, the warehouse has no use for them. But rather than throw them away, Target "recycles" them to nonprofit organizations that can use them. To run this large-scale operation, Target has hired Project for Pride in Living (PPL), a nonprofit agency that teaches disabled people job skills. PPL trainees pick up the samples, sort them, match them with nonprofit requests, and deliver the goods to recipient organizations. This continuing contract between Target and PPL provides necessary training for PPL clients and a needed service for the company at a reasonable cost.

A Hewlett-Packard sales office in Englewood, Colorado, has also found a novel way of disposing of waste. In this case, the waste is the Styrofoam peanuts used in packing. The sales center, which receives regular shipments of computer equipment from the factories, was overflowing with the peanuts. While everyone said, "We can't just throw them away!", no one knew what to do with them—until one day, when someone came up with a bright idea. Why not give them to a nonprofit organization, which could turn around and sell them to a mailing house, generating a profit for itself? That's exactly what the sales office did. It now gives its peanuts to the local Boy Scouts, who sell them to Mail Boxes Etc. and other mailing companies. The profit is spent on scholarships to send needy boys to summer Scout camp.

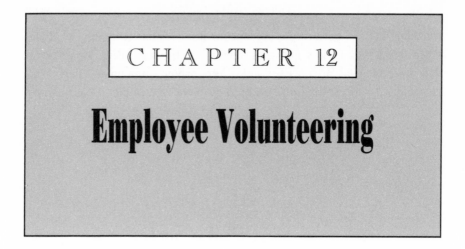

CHAPTER 12

Employee Volunteering

Much too often, nonprofit organizations serving the community have more work than staff or money. In such cases, these groups may find themselves with extremely worthwhile projects that cannot be completed because of a lack of personnel.

—from "Community Service at IBM"

One of the biggest gifts corporations can give to nonprofits is *people*: corporate employees as volunteers. Nonprofits rely on volunteers to carry out many of their programs and they rarely have enough, so the arrival of a motivated, committed crew of workers can be as good as cash.

The gift of volunteers also benefits the corporation. Peter Drucker—the respected author, management consultant, and college professor—suggests that companies use employee volunteer programs as tools for management training, because they help employees hone their skills in managing and motivating people. Companies with active volunteer programs also find that their employees enjoy the opportunity to give time and effort to an organization: they like the feeling of contributing to society and return to work motivated and "refreshed."

Participating in a corporate volunteer program also makes employees feel good about the company. Surveys have shown that employees prefer to work for companies that participate in community service. The knowledge that a company cares about the community tends to inspire loyalty and pride.

Corporate volunteers run the gamut from skilled to unskilled, short-term to long-term. They include people from every level of a corporation, working independently or in teams. Although most companies urge employees to volunteer their own time, many release workers to help nonprofits on the company clock. In short, the rules governing employee volunteer programs are as diverse as the companies that run them. Only three rules of thumb seem to guide the successful ones: let employees drive the program, let them pick the agencies they will serve, and be sincere—commit to the program, talk about it in company newsletters, help employees find agencies to work for, recognize employees who volunteer.

The following programs have been chosen to illustrate the range of possibilities.

Target Stores: A Team Approach to Volunteering

Target Stores, a division of Dayton Hudson Corporation, has a strong commitment to making its communities healthy places in which to live and raise a family. One of the ways Target Stores expresses that commitment is by actively encouraging employee volunteers. The Good Neighbor Program, administered from the company's corporate headquarters in Minneapolis as part of its corporate giving program, has an annual budget of $250,000, which is spent to support employee volunteer efforts in each of the company's locations.

The Good Neighbor Program emphasizes the use of teams of Target employees to solve community problems. The choice of problem and solution is left to local employees. The one stipulation: employees must work together on a project of mutual consent. Projects range from the March of Dimes Walk America pledge drive, for which many Target Stores provide teams of walkers; to "paint-a-thons" in which teams of Target employees paint the houses of elderly citizens; to "adopt-a-school" programs in which teams of workers tutor children, organize carnivals, chaperone field trips, and build playground equipment. For some projects—such as walk-a-thons—Target volunteers join efforts that have been coordinated by other organizations. Other projects—such as "adopting" a sheltered workshop—are wholly initiated by Target volunteers. Projects can be one-day events or long-term partnerships. Employees do their volunteering on their own time; headquarters urges each Target location to do at least one volunteer project a year. Virtually every location participates. Some do the bare minimum; most do more; some do as many as fifty projects.

To help them select projects, headquarters provides each location with employee preference forms. Employees use these forms to note their volunteering choices (type of agency, type of work, available hours, etc.). Then, at each location, a Good Neighbor Captain compiles the information and finds local causes that meet the employees' needs. Because the emphasis is on teamwork, the onus is on the captain to find projects that will please a group of workers—and on the workers to compromise if their own favorite project isn't chosen.

The captain, too, is a volunteer. Target has not given the job to the store manager or personnel manager for a number of reasons. First, the company wants to avoid "dumping" the job on someone who is overloaded or doesn't want it. Second, it wants to spread responsibility for the program to regular employees. In a program that is highly democratic and driven by employee interests, Target believes employee management is important. It's also educational. Good Neighbor Captains must locate community projects, coordinate sometimes conflicting employee desires, and manage volunteer supplies and schedules. To help them in this sometimes time-consuming task, headquarters lets them make their arrangements on company time. It also gives them a Good Neighbor Guidebook, a three-ring binder that contains everything a captain needs to know to run a successful program. The guidebook contains suggestions for projects, tips on recognizing volunteers, suggestions for generating visibility in the store and in the community, and other "how to" information. Headquarters also asks captains to record information about their projects so that the company can track the efforts of its volunteers. The company then disseminates suggestions from one location to another about successful volunteer efforts.

Why Teamwork?

Why does Target require teamwork rather than individual volunteering? For several reasons. The company believes that by working together, employees build a spirit of teamwork that carries over into the workplace. The company also believes that by sending teams of Target workers out into the community, it builds the company's presence there. Teams of Target workers, all wearing Target T-shirts, make a strong statement that Target Stores cares about its neighbors.

T-shirts are about as far as the company goes to generate publicity about the program. The Good Neighbor Guidebook contains sample press releases which employees (sometimes) ask their nonprofit partners to give to the press. It also contains suggestions for activities or displays employees can set up inside the store to publicize the volunteer programs. But frequently these are not done. The company could put more effort into publicity, but chooses not to, seeing the program as a community service rather than a promotional effort.

Employee Response

Employee response to the program has been strong. The company has found that getting a local program off the ground is sometimes a challenge, but that once a program is running, enthusiasm tends to spread like wildfire. The positive nature of the work, the chance to meet new people and try new things, and the feeling of making a difference all seem to bolster people's spirits. If the number of project suggestions is any indication, employee support for the program is high. When the program manager asked the captains if they needed help finding projects, the resounding answer was no. Finding projects wasn't the problem. It was winnowing the list that was the challenge.

IBM: Paid Release Time

IBM has long been known for its community service efforts. The Community Service Assignments program is one of the reasons. The program enables IBM employees to volunteer full-time, for up to a year, for a qualifying nonprofit, with full salary and benefits paid. Why is the company so generous? Because it believes that the community, the employee, and the company all benefit.

Matching Employees to Nonprofits

Employees are loaned to nonprofits in one of three ways: an employee may request an assignment, a nonprofit may request an employee, or the company may be aware of a nonprofit's need and offer to lend an employee in response. The majority of assignments happen at the employee's request. Most often, employees who are actively involved in a nonprofit, already donating significant amounts of their own time, ask for an assignment. The employee must make a case for the assignment to his or her manager. The manager reviews the arguments and makes a decision. Although a report is filed with IBM headquarters in Armonk, New York, the decision rests with the manager.

What does a manager look for? Several things. He or she examines the type of assignment the employee is requesting. IBM prefers to place employees in positions that have a "multiplier effect"—that is, provide a continuing benefit to the organization even after the employee has left. One example is the development and implementation of a planning process which the nonprofit will use for years to come. The company also prefers positions that focus on a special project with clearly defined goals, rather than positions in day-to-day operations. The manager looks for signs of employee commitment—evidence that the employee has worked for the organization on his or her own time and genuinely wants to contribute. Finally the manager discusses with the employee strategies for handling the person's workload in his or her absence. Sometimes an IBM'er is brought in from another department; occasionally an outsider is hired. Ultimately, if the manager believes that the nonprofit's needs, the employee's skills, and the company's business requirements are compatible, he or she will recommend the assignment.

Assignments generally last a year, although shorter assignments are made. They include a wide range of skills and responsibilities, but the majority involve helping the nonprofit gain business and management expertise. For example, a junior personnel officer spent six months working for the international relief agency Save the Children, where she strengthened the volunteer recruiting system. A technical support manager worked as director of a small nonprofit community development agency, where he doubled the agency's clientele and income. Some employees learn so much from their assignments that they return to IBM in more senior positions. The majority, however, return to the same or similar jobs.

The assignment program is open to employees at all levels. Although no criteria govern who can apply, most applicants are upper-level managers who have been with the company for a long time. They have usually been with the nonprofit for a long time as well, and have specific skills they wish to offer.

Criteria for nonprofits are only a little more strict. To receive an employee, a nonprofit must be a tax-exempt organization. Its purpose must be to provide "a material service" to society. It may not be a religious or political organization or one that supports a position on a highly controversial issue. Conflict-of-interest situations, in which an assignment would involve the choice or installation of computer equipment, are also ineligible.

Why Does IBM Do It?

Why does the company encourage employees to leave for a year with full pay and benefits? The answer lies in IBM's corporate culture. "We serve our interests best when we serve the public interest," says a corporate brochure, and we get the sense, when talking with IBM employees, that the company really means it. We asked over and over again, "Why is IBM so generous? Why for a year? Why full pay?'' Over and over again we heard the same response: "It's part of our culture to give back to the community.''

To understand this, it's important to understand first that IBM believes that the health of the company and the health of the community are inextricably related. A decaying community will not provide good workers or consumers for the corporation. It is in the company's best interest to contribute directly to the health of its surroundings. IBM sees itself as a world leader in this regard. And it backs up its vision with action.

Second, the company believes that employees benefit from volunteering. They develop new skills and strengthen old ones. They come back refreshed. And because the employees benefit, the company benefits—not necessarily from specific skills gained; the company has no expectation of a tangible return. Rather, the improved morale and energy the employees bring with them has a salutary effect on the rest of the company.

For these reasons, IBM is committed to this program. It has assigned more than a thousand employees since the program began in 1971. Requests and assignments "bubble up from the sites" at the rate of approximately fifty a year. Employees whose requests are turned down can turn to the Faculty Loan Program or to Personal Community Service, two other IBM volunteer programs.

With its massive work force, worldwide operations, corporate stature, and financial clout, IBM can afford a program this generous. Such efforts are harder for smaller, less established companies. Nonetheless, the Community Service Assignments program is an inspiring model for other companies that really want to make a difference in their communities.

Nations Bank: Two Hours a Week to Help at School

Nations Bank, with branches in 700 communities in nine states, is very much a local bank. That's because all of its communities are different. With branches in Dallas as well as in Cashiers, North Carolina, the bank must respond to a broad range of community needs and an equally broad range of employee concerns.

One thing that unifies this diverse group, however, is that the bank's work force is predominantly female. That means a lot of employees balancing the demands of work and family. To meet their needs, the bank created a work/family program in the early 1980s which offers extended parental leave, flex-time and job-sharing, child-care referral, and other services.

By the mid-eighties the bank was aware of growing pressure to address the problems of schools. Schools were a big issue for employees, who needed time to talk with teachers, attend meetings, and respond to their children's needs. They were also a big issue in each of the bank's communities. Test scores were declining. Class sizes were increasing. The flood of women into the work force had robbed schools of volunteers. Schools were asking the bank for help. The bank wanted to respond, but how? Throwing money at the problem didn't seem effective: with a presence in 700 communities, the bank could give only a minimal amount to any single school or district.

It would be more effective, the bank realized, to offer *people*: employee volunteers. This would restore some of the volunteers lost by women's move to the workplace. It would provide tangible help and skills the schools badly needed. It would meet needs in every one of the bank's communities. And it would address pressing concerns of employees.

So in 1989 the bank initiated an employee school volunteer program. Employees are released for two hours a week to volunteer in a school of their choice. Some volunteer in their own children's school; others join teams of employees who jointly adopt a school. They work as teacher's aides, as one-on-one tutors, as athletic coaches. Some who have particular management or administrative expertise take on special projects such as helping computerize a school. Some use the time to visit their own children's teachers or attend school meetings. The program is open to all full-time employees, and workers are actively encouraged to take part. The program is described in the employee handbook and covered in orientation sessions. It is also discussed regularly in the employee newsletter, which prints stories about volunteers and their activities.

Why Two Hours?

Why two hours off for volunteering? The bank believed that employees could give two hours a week without getting behind in their work and without burdening other employees. It would give employees in big cities thirty minutes to commute each way and still leave a solid hour for work in a classroom. Workers in smaller areas could get in as much as an hour and a half at the school.

The bank purposely encouraged volunteering during the workday because it wanted employees to know how seriously it takes the program. The bank reinforced its commitment by expanding the one-to-one employee matching gifts program to include kindergarten through high school, in addition to the college program the bank already had in place.

And what has been the employee response? Two years into the program, Nations Bank has not done any formal tracking to learn how many participate. The bank knows that 300 employees out of approximately 4,000 at its Charlotte headquarters have teamed up to adopt a single elementary school. It doesn't know how many others are volunteering on their own. Verbal response, however, has been extremely positive.

CHAPTER 13

In-Kind Donations

We at L'eggs Products, Inc., have certainly realized what a smart investment in-kind giving is. Over the past few years, it has helped us trim inventory, increase productivity, free warehouse space, and subsequently reduce the cost of storing inventory.

—L'eggs Products, Inc.

From used items a company no longer needs to current inventory a company can no longer sell, the list of things a company can donate to a nonprofit is long. So is the list of reasons for doing so. First, there are tax benefits. Companies that donate used products can often deduct the fair market value of the items. Companies that donate current unsold inventory can deduct even more. They can take a "stepped up" deduction, which equals the cost of making the product plus half the difference between its retail price and its cost (up to twice the retail price). For example, if you donate an item that cost $50 to manufacture and sells for $100, you can deduct $75.

Second, there are inventory control benefits. Donating products to nonprofits can save a company warehousing costs as well as inventory carrying costs and can help a company dispose of out-of-date products without destroying or liquidating them.

Third, there are public relations benefits. As with any other type of partnership, donations can be made strategically—to groups in your geographic area, for instance, or to certain types of agencies. In this way they can be used to reinforce marketing goals.

Fourth, there are philanthropic benefits. Giving products to a non-profit helps the nonprofit in its work—sometimes even more than an equivalent amount of cash.

The spectrum of "donatables" is broad. It includes products in current inventory as well as ones that would otherwise be liquidated or thrown away. It includes services companies perform as their major line of business, as well as services they perform for their own use. The following stories describe a variety of in-kind donation programs and the benefits they bring to the nonprofit recipients as well as their corporate donors.

Apple Computer: Donating Current Inventory

In 1983 Apple created a corporate giving program called Kids Can't Wait. The point of the program was to put an Apple computer into every California school. Was it philanthropy? Absolutely. The computers were tax-deductible. Was it marketing? It certainly was. Apple knew that by giving computers to teachers and students, it was building a market for its products.

Now the surprising news: after several years the company ended the program and shifted the focus of its giving away from a marketing slant. Apple still gives computers—lots of them. It still gives them to schools. But the focus of the program and the benefits to the company are now very different. How come?

Apple shut down Kids Can't Wait for a very specific reason. As the company looked back at the schools that had received computers, it found that many of the machines were sitting in closets. People didn't know how to use them. Without a system for providing technical support, the gifts were nice gestures—but useless. Useless to the recipients; equally useless to Apple in terms of generating future sales. So the company decided to move away from "big gesture" gifts and to concentrate instead on giving to a smaller number of recipients in a more in-depth way.

Today Apple's donation program is virtually the antithesis of Kids Can't Wait. In Crossroads, Apple's flagship school donation program, the company limits the number of recipients to twenty a year and then works extensively with those groups to develop their projects. The company targets underserved populations—schools in rural areas and inner cities. And it selects groups that are proposing highly innovative projects. For instance, a school in Newark, New Jersey, got Macintoshes so that kids could desktop-publish a magazine. An inner-city school in San Diego used computers for monitoring air quality. The grant period lasts for three years, with Apple initially giving the group a small number of machines, then evaluating their use, and then giving a larger number of units once the program is off the ground.

Another focus of Apple's giving program is the Earthgrants program. In 1990 Apple decided to become a "green" company, to make its manufacturing and packaging environmentally sound. In keeping with that goal, the company targeted universities and colleges for gifts of computers that are used for unusual environmental projects. As with the Crossroads program, the company is pushing its grantees to develop high-end uses for the machines, to stretch the computers beyond their ordinary applications.

The community affairs department at Apple, which operates the computer grants program, is adamant that the program is purely philanthropic. The company believes it has a responsibility to treat its employees and the community well. Does that mean there's no return to the company for its largesse? Hardly. The programs build loyalty with computer users. They promote an image of the company as a caring and generous citizen. And they develop multiple new uses for Apple equipment. The company isn't shy about promoting those uses. Grantees are regularly asked to speak to the press, to present at seminars, to disseminate the results of their projects. By showcasing their work, Apple not only shows off its generosity, but it shows the world the powerful things its computers can do.

Livingston & Company: Donating a Service

Livingston & Company is a small advertising agency in Seattle, best known for a series of clever, eyecatching billboards it designs for Seattle's Museum of Flight. Even more surprising than the billboards themselves is that they are designed for free as part of Livingston's longstanding commitment to doing pro bono work for local nonprofits. The zoo, the aquarium, the Seattle Indian Health Board, and other organizations have all received substantial in-kind services from the agency. Why does Livingston do this? Why does it donate time—its stock in trade—when it could easily fill the time with paying clients? For two reasons. First, the agency wants to give something back to the community. Second, it gets a very direct return.

The return is actually twofold. The agency knows that the best way to generate paying work is to do high-visibility ads. That's exactly what its nonprofit partners let it do. Unlike corporate clients who place constraints on the agency, the pro bono clients let the art directors have free rein. The result is a series of ads that command attention, that make people stop and ask, "Who did that?" Making the situation even more advantageous, the ads often appear on donated billboards, where they are highly visible in the community. "So," said Pat Doody, Livingston's office manager, "we love the pro bono work. It's the best way we could advertise the agency."

The second benefit of the pro bono program is that Livingston employees love it. The ads are fun to do. They're a wonderful diversion from the more conventional work the agency does for its corporate clients. And, said Doody, "nonprofits don't look a gift horse in the mouth and then extract its molars. They're getting the work for free. They usually just say 'Thank you.' "

How much time does the company give to its freebies? The work tends to come in concentrated periods. Five or six people may spend 15 to 20 percent of their time on a job before it's finished. They try not to go over 20 percent. Occasionally projects will come at exactly the wrong time, when the agency is overloaded with paid work on deadlines. "But that's the nature of our business," said Doody. "It's not too tough to handle."

Although Livingston donates creative time for the ads, the nonprofits pay to have them produced. But thanks to a little arm-twisting by the agency, placement of most of the ads is free. Local billboard, radio, TV, and transit space is donated. (Only newspapers insist on payment.) In fact, Ackerley Communications, which owns all the local billboards, has been especially receptive to the pro bono campaigns— also for business-building reasons. Ackerley would rather fill an empty spot with an attention-grabbing billboard than with a sign that says "Your ad here." Like Livingston, the company believes people driving by will notice and say, "Hey, I want a billboard like that for my business."

Starbuck's, Harbor Properties, et al.: Donating Waste Products

Some nonprofits virtually owe their existence to corporate waste. This is especially true for food banks, which receive a portion of their foodstuffs from individuals, but get the lion's share from food processors and retailers. Most of the food donated is mislabeled or otherwise improperly packaged. It may be unfit for commercial sale, but it provides the backbone of feeding programs for hungry and homeless people nationwide. On a smaller, local level, Starbuck's Coffee, a national retailer, with headquarters in Seattle, prides itself on selling only the freshest beans. It gives its older beans to local food banks, which are happy to serve the classy brew to their clients.

For the majority of nonprofits, office equipment and supplies top the list of desirable gifts. Corporations tend to update equipment fairly regularly, but many nonprofits are still slugging out memos on electric typewriters. Donations of older but usable computers, calculators, and other equipment can save them hours of labor as well as hundreds or thousands of dollars. The same is true for furnishings. While many companies favor offices with coordinated decor, most nonprofits decorate with vintage Goodwill. And even those purchases can strain a budget by taking money from other projects.

Harbor Properties, a Seattle commercial real estate developer, routinely "recycles" the carpeting it pulls out of office buildings when refurbishing for new tenants. It offers the old carpets to local nonprofits, which are delighted with the donations. Similarly, Seattle-based Rainier Bank (now part of BankAmerica) periodically replaces its office furniture. It gives the "old" furniture to local nonprofits, which save thousands of dollars in furnishing costs.

Puget Power, Metropolitan Life: Donating an In-House Service

Some companies find that donating to a nonprofit benefits the company as much as the nonprofit. Puget Power, a utility company serving communities in western Washington state, has a large in-house print shop which prints statement inserts, annual reports, and other materials for the company. Most of the time, company business keeps the state-of-the-art equipment humming. But occasionally work is slow. Rather than have the machines and technicians sit idle, the company takes in print jobs for local nonprofits. The nonprofits love it, since it saves them hundreds of dollars in printing bills. The print shop loves it as well—in fact, those are their favorite jobs. The print shop manager told us: "They're more interesting than our regular work. They push us a little bit."

Donating a service can also take the pain out of saying no. Metropolitan Life Insurance Company has long partnered the American Society on Aging (ASA). Met Life has loaned executives to ASA's Business Forum on Aging, a committee of businesses concerned about the rapid aging of America and the effects on business. And Met Life has funded numerous publications and workshops held by the organization. When ASA approached Met Life for money to produce an educational videotape on aging, the company was feeling pinched and felt compelled to say no. However, it came up with something it could say yes to: the loan of its in-house video production facilities. Met Life produced the video for ASA, giving it a better finished product than the organization had originally budgeted for and contributing more in kind than the agency had requested in cash.

Clearinghouses for In-Kind Donations

Companies that want to donate products to a nonprofit, but don't want the hassle of administering a program, can use a clearinghouse. Gifts in Kind America and the National Association for the Exchange of Industrial Resources (NAEIR) are just two organizations that provide this service. Both are nonprofits themselves, and both develop giving programs for companies on a turnkey basis. Together they help approximately two thousand companies a year donate current inventory to nonprofit organizations. They donate software packages for Microsoft, shoes for Nike, clothing for K Mart, personal care products for Gillette, and numerous other products for other *Fortune* 500 and smaller companies. Some of their donations represent excess inventory, a one-time surplus a company needs to dispose of. Other items are part of a long-term giving program of a corporation that is administered by the clearinghouse. The companies refer requests for donations directly to the clearinghouse, which processes the requests, arranges the shipping, provides the required tax documentation, and even handles the publicity. This turnkey service is free to the corporate donors. Costs are covered by the nonprofit recipients, who pay shipping and handling fees as well as a yearly membership fee. Gifts in Kind America also receives donations from United Way and foundations.

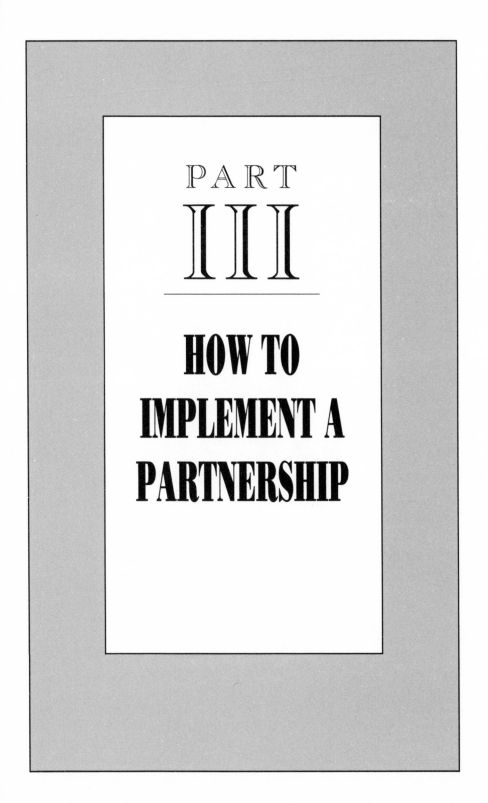

PART

III

HOW TO IMPLEMENT A PARTNERSHIP

CHAPTER 14

Ground Rules: Things to Consider Before You Begin

Business is a combination of war and sport.

—André Maurois, *The Life of Disraeli*

Conducting a public purpose partnership is a lot like playing volleyball at the company picnic. It takes people from different departments, puts them all in one place, tosses a strange ball into their laps, and then expects them to act like a team. The remarkable thing is that it often works. In most companies, by the end of the first quarter, people have learned each other's moves. By half-time they've developed a strategy for winning. And by the end of the game, they've learned to meld their separate strengths into some pretty solid teamwork.

Of course, there's a key difference between volleyball and partnerships. At the company picnic you're left to your own devices with just a six-pack to smooth the teamwork and get you through the game. For a partnership you've actually got a players' manual—this book— to help you devise a winning strategy. We can't make you into seasoned players, but we *can* give you the benefit of other teams' experience. We can help you develop goals for your program. We can help you design its elements so that they meet the greatest number of needs. And we can help you work with a nonprofit partner so that when the ball is in your partner's court you know what to expect. We can walk you through the process so that when your first partnership is over, you'll feel you handled the ball well.

Commitment to the Game

Don't even think about entering into a partnership if management doesn't support the idea. It takes too much time, too much effort, too much rewriting of rules. It won't fly unless upper management has given its full support. Now, that doesn't mean that upper management should be involved in all decisions. Operating decisions are best left to people in the departments that are carrying out the program. But management commitment to the *strategy* of public purpose partnering is vital for the program to succeed.

Take the Long View

Preferably, that commitment should be long-term—longer than just one program. After all, your first program may not work. Or it may work, but not as well as you'd hoped. You're learning. You're building new behaviors, new ways of working across departments, new ways of evaluating what you do. We'll talk in Chapter 19, "Piggyback Ventures," about making your first venture a pilot program—about implementing it, evaluating it, and then deciding how to proceed. But ideally, even before you begin, management should be committed to the strategy and should realize that the big payoff is down the road. That's tough in our "this quarter" economy. But you're building long-term goodwill. You're forging a long-term relationship with customers. You're achieving long-term social gains. You need to support that with a long-term strategy.

Give It Adequate Resources

Management needs to commit not only time to the program, but also resources. That means money, people, importance—*a mandate*. Management must provide the mandate that makes everybody give the program what it needs.

It may need a lot. For example, a partnership may draw on people from many departments. Management must mandate that people be freed to work on it. A partnership demands start-up capital, probably from several different budgets. Management must mandate the allotment of those funds. A partnership frequently requires additional cash once it's underway. Management must mandate that additional cash be available. Management is like the team owner. Team members may squabble; coaches may argue over strategies and use of funds. Management's role is to remain above the fray, to think for the long term, to stand behind the program so that it gets what it needs.

Give It Room to Maneuver

Public purpose partnering involves breaking rules. Marketing and Human Resources don't usually work together? Fine. In public purpose partnering they do. Your corporate giving programs are not evaluated for a bottom-line return? Fine. In public purpose partnership they may be. Your corporate communications programs must absolutely, positively live within their budgets? Fine. Partnership programs may get more leeway.

In public purpose partnering you're doing things your company has never done before. You're learning on the fly. You're making up the rules as you go along. Your program needs the freedom to do that. It needs permission to make mistakes. It needs permission to miss a deadline: you've never worked with a nonprofit before. It needs permission to borrow staff and money from other departments: you didn't know you needed those things until—well, until you needed them.

Your public purpose effort should be treated like an enterprise unit within the larger organization: free from some of the usual operating constraints; coddled a little so that it has room to grow; free to borrow

resources where it becomes necessary. Management must give it this
room to maneuver to give it room to succeed.

Building the Team

The Starting Lineup

While your partnership program will benefit many parts of the organization, it must be managed by a relatively small group of people.
These core players should represent the three functions that will be
most directly involved: marketing, corporate giving, and human relations. (In some companies one person may wear more than one of
these hats.) With support from upper management, these people
should be charged with developing a partnership philosophy and setting the strategy in motion.

Who should the core players be? One or two people from each
department will be adequate—but the choice of people is crucial. They
should be high enough in the hierarchy to have power. You want
decision-makers, not rubber-stampers—budget-controllers, not
approval-seekers. When the team is in a room together, it must be
able to make decisions—even financial decisions—without chains of
approval above it. At least one person must have easy access to top
management so that when an executive decision is needed, it can be
obtained quickly. These people must all believe in the program, and
understand the ''big picture'' benefits to the corporation. They must
want to be on the team and must be willing to give it the time it needs.
They may need to be freed from some other responsibilities in order
to do so.

The Bench

This core team of people will need to bring in players from other
departments at various stages in the partnership process.

Initially, they will need input from numerous people as they frame
goals for the program. Every area that stands to benefit must be

consulted. While the list will vary from corporation to corporation, it will probably include advertising, community affairs, government affairs, business development, research and development, and others. People from these departments should be involved in framing overall goals for the program, and in setting goals for individual campaigns that will benefit their departments.

Individual campaigns will involve other departments to greater or lesser degrees. For a campaign that involves the company's sales force and franchisees, representatives from the sales department will be added to the team. For a campaign that involves partnering a non-profit on a local community issue, representatives from community affairs will come on board. For a campaign that links a new product or service with a nonprofit partner, representatives from the business development office will get involved. Advertising and public relations people will join the team for almost all campaigns to plan the campaigns' ad and PR strategies. The core team must be free to call on players from other departments as their skills are needed, and as those departments stand to benefit.

Team Captain

The team will include many people from many departments working on many projects besides your public purpose partnership. To keep this ball rolling, one person will need to coordinate. This person's job will be to stay on top of the process, to shepherd it from start to finish. He or she will need to call the meetings, keep the schedule, and do the myriad tasks, large and small, that coordinating a complex, cross-departmental project requires. Who this person is will be crucial to the success of the project.

- The person must be creative and energetic: he should love the challenge of doing new things because he'll be writing the rules as he goes along.
- The person must be experienced at corporate politics: she'll

ROLES AND RESPONSIBILITIES IN CAUSE-RELATED MARKETING

Position	Initiates	Approves	Develops	Implements	Evaluates
CORPORATE					
CEO/PRESIDENT	○	◐	○	○	◐
VP OF MARKETING	◐	●	◐	●	●
MARKETING/BRAND MANAGER	●	●	●	●	●
DIRECTOR OF PROMOTION	◐	●	●	●	◐
DIRECTOR OF ADVERTISING	○	◐	◐	●	○
DIRECTOR OF SALES	○	○	◐	●	◐
DIRECTOR OF PR/COMMUNITY RELATIONS	○	◐	○	○	○
CHARITY					
EXECUTIVE DIRECTOR	○	●	○	○	●
DEVELOPMENT DIRECTOR	◐	●	◐	●	●
FINANCIAL DIRECTOR	○	◐	○	○	●
FOUNDATION					
PRESIDENT/DIRECTOR	○	○	○	○	○
OUTSIDE AGENCIES/CONSULTANTS					
ADVERTISING	○	○	◐	●	○
PROMOTIONAL	●	○	●	●	◐

LEVEL OF INVOLVEMENT: ● HEAVY ◐ MODERATE ○ NONE

*Used with permission of Sheridan Associates.

have to know how to skirt the customary rules and how to convince key players to act.

• The person must be persuasive and respected: he'll have to defend the program to naysayers and sell it to fence-sitters.

• The person must have clout: as she goes through the company asking for money, staff, and input, she'll need the weight of upper management behind her so that she can get the program what it needs.

• The person must have time to do the job: he should be relieved of other tasks if necessary, because no one else will have this as a top priority and the momentum of the project will ride on his shoulders.

• Most of all, the team captain should love the program. He or she must believe in the program and its benefit to the company and the community, because in the long run enthusiasm will be his or her best sales tool.

Referee

Your corporate giving representatives should work most closely with your nonprofit partners. They are used to working with nonprofits; they speak their language; they understand their needs. They will be valuable brokers between the nonprofit's culture and yours. Take advantage of that! Let them take the lead in identifying nonprofits to work with. Let them make the initial contacts. Let them run the meetings at which both partners are present. Once you've developed working relationships with your nonprofit partners, that will no longer be necessary. But it's a good insurance policy in the early days of the program.

Be Sincere

One last piece of advice—one that we've given you before but that bears repeating—before you get on with your game plan: don't undertake public purpose partnering unless you really believe in your chosen cause. If you're insincere, it will be apparent to consumers and your campaign will backfire. Witness the case of Sandhurst Farms, a dairy in Australia that launched a marketing campaign ostensibly designed to educate the public about the dangers of osteoporosis. The campaign quoted the Arthritis Foundation extensively in print and television ads, emphasizing the seriousness of the disease and the need to increase calcium consumption to combat it. This would have been fine had the company actually partnered the Arthritis Foundation in developing the campaign. But it hadn't. Sandhurst had never spoken with anyone at the foundation, nor had the foundation endorsed the campaign. The ads were quickly recognized as a blatant attempt to capitalize on a troubling disease, and as a deceitful way to sell milk. The ad campaign was withdrawn, but not before the company's credibility had been seriously impaired.

The lesson: believe in your cause. Believe that by helping it you help yourself. Design your campaign accordingly.

CHAPTER 15

Setting Goals

Unfortunately, this is a true story. Among our corporate partners at the Denver Children's Museum was a toy store. The store's owners asked us to develop a booklet about toys you can make at home. They wanted to offer it as a premium for parents. So we worked up a nifty little booklet, full of activities parents and kids could do together to turn everyday objects into fun and games. The store's owners loved it. So did kids and parents. In fact, after using the booklet for several months, the store decided to sell it rather than give it away. The store didn't want to charge a lot; it just wanted to cover its costs. The store was buying the booklets from the museum for $.13 each. It planned to sell each book for $.15, which it figured would cover the cost of the book, along with a $.02 pencil bearing the store's name. The store planned to sell the two together, tied with a ribbon. When we pointed out to the store's owners that it would actually lose money on this deal, since it wasn't taking into account the cost of staff time to pick up the booklets at the museum, stock them, and tie the pencils on, not to mention the cost of the ribbon, the store owners said unabashedly, "Oh, that's OK. These booklets are moving so fast, we'll make it up in volume!"

Now, you may laugh at this story. Your company wouldn't make such an obvious mistake. The surprising thing is that many companies do

make an equally basic mistake when it comes to public purpose partnership campaigns. They fail to think realistically about why they're
engaging in them and what they want to get out of it.

Setting Goals for Your Partnership

The first task of your partnership team is to determine why the
company is doing a public purpose partnership. That sounds elementary: you're doing it because it's good for business and good for the
community! Well, that's a good start, but it's not enough. For your
program to succeed, you need well-thought-out goals and expectations, and those goals and expectations must be shared by all members of the team.

Getting the Most Out of It

A lot of companies that do public purpose partnering unwittingly
shortchange themselves. They think of the partnership exclusively as
a marketing program. They expect it to create excitement at the retail
level and to produce short-term sales gains. They're right: partnerships should do that. But they can do a lot more. The real goal of
partnering is to produce numerous *long-term* gains for the company:
gains in corporate reputation, customer retention, employee recruitment, employee morale, community strength, maybe even government policies. The list is almost as long as the number of departments
in your organization. By including them all in the goal-setting process,
you can design a program that may help meet their needs.

So the first step in setting goals for your program is to ask each
department about its own goals. One or more members of your team
should meet with representatives from other areas to talk about their
goals. Start with marketing, corporate giving, and human relations; then
work out toward community affairs, new business development, and
others. You'll probably find overlaps among them. Good! Those are areas

that lend themselves to partnership campaigns. In fact, chances are that as your team pools the lists, ideas for campaigns will start to appear.

Marketing Goals

It makes sense to start with your marketing goals because if you're like most companies, your partnership campaign will have a strong marketing component.

Setting Overall Goals

Your company has numerous marketing goals: you market your overall company image; you market individual products or services; you may also market a product or service line. You may market to a single consumer group or to several groups with different characteristics. Each of these marketing goals has its own challenges, and you'll need to decide which ones you want to tie to a partnership campaign. For starters, look at each distinct group of marketing goals and ask yourselves the following questions:

1. For each of our products or services . . .
   - what geographic markets are we trying to reach?
   - what socioeconomic markets?
   - what gender?
   - what age group?
   - what life-style characteristics?
   - what ethnic group?

   What other characteristics distinguish our target consumers?
2. What are our goals for each of these target markets?
   - to get them to try our product or service?
   - to encourage them to become or remain regular customers?
   - to encourage them to buy from our store, from other stores, by catalog, by phone?
   - to get them to tell friends about our product or service?

What other goals do we have for our target markets?

3. How do we want buyers to think about each of our products or services? What three words do we want them to associate with each product or service?
4. Where do we currently go to reach these people? Which campaigns have worked, and why? Which have failed, and why?
5. Do we have middlemen who help us get our product or service to the customer? If so, what are our goals for them?
   - to get them excited about the product or service?
   - to get them to give us more space? more attention?

   What other goals do we have for them?
6. How do we want people to think about our company? What five words do we want people to associate with us?

Tying Goals to a Partnership Program

Your partnership campaign can't help you meet all these goals, so you'll need to pinpoint the ones you want to tie to the campaign. Two factors will help you decide: marketing needs with particular urgency, and the ease with which certain products or services lend themselves to this kind of campaign. Ask yourselves the following questions:

1. Is there one product or service that could use a boost right now?

Partnerships can be a good way to focus attention on a particular product or service, so if one is lagging, this might be the way to give it a shove—especially if it has a natural fit with a social issue or a nonprofit.

Alice's, a restaurant in Seattle, wanted a way to highlight its new breakfast service, so it launched a cause-related marketing campaign with a local food bank. Newspaper ads and table tents advertised that the restaurant would give 5 percent of every breakfast tab to the food bank for an unspecified period. Alice's believes that the campaign was one factor that helped get the new breakfast business off to a strong start. It also strengthened the restaurant's image as a good community citizen.

The disadvantage of tying a partnership campaign to a single product or service is that the campaign will cost as much as a campaign that features an entire product line or the entire corporate image, making it less efficient as a marketing expense. But if that's where your needs are, it's probably worth the cost.

2. Where is the best natural fit between your company and a social cause? Is it a single product or service? a line of products or services? or the whole company's image?

For a marketing partnership to work, the fit between the company and the cause must seem natural. There should be some logical, immediately apparent connection between your business and the work of your nonprofit partner.

For example, Ralston Purina makes pet foods, breakfast cereals, and flashlights. What social cause would fit with all those products? None! So doing a partnership campaign around the entire product line or the whole company image made no sense. On the other hand, each product line suggested a logical fit with a particular cause or nonprofit: pet foods with the Humane Society (appealing to pet owners), cereals with the American Heart Association (emphasizing their healthfulness), and Eveready flashlights with the Red Cross (helpful in emergencies). The company fashioned three separate cause-related marketing campaigns, one around each product line.

Philanthropic Goals

Your philanthropic goals will obviously play a significant role in shaping your partnership program. If your company has a history of giving money, you probably already have standards in place for donations. You may even have existing relationships with nonprofits or social issues that lend themselves to a campaign. You'll have to decide how much you want your program to be influenced by those practices. Like philanthropy, public purpose partnerships benefit nonprofits. But they are also business-building programs. Therefore, you are free to make up new rules.

If your company lacks a systematic corporate giving strategy, this

is a good time to think about one. The following questions can help
you structure both a philanthropic program and a partnership.

1. To whom do we give money now?
   - To what social causes?
   - To what nonprofits?
   - Do we have repeat recipients, or are all recipients new each
     year?
   - How were these choices made?
2. To whom do we want to be giving money?
   - To what social causes?
   - In what geographic region(s)?
   - Are there specific nonprofits we've targeted?
   - Why?
3. Is our philanthropy "strategic"?
   - Is it done purely for social benefit, with no expected return
     to the company?
   - Is it done with an eye on the corporate bottom line?
   - Is it somewhere in between?
4. Is our philanthropy effective?
   - Do we evaluate its results?
   - Does it produce the desired benefit to the company and to
     the recipients?
5. Are there restrictions on our use of philanthropy dollars? What
   are they?
6. Can we make our philanthropy more strategic within the limits
   of our restrictions?
   - Can we link it to our target markets?
   - Can we involve our employees?
7. What individuals must be involved in philanthropic decisions?
   How do they feel about strategic philanthropy and partnerships?

Human Resources

Think of your partnership campaign as a tool for building employee morale. It gives your workers a chance to participate in something fun, a chance to contribute to a social cause, and a chance to feel proud of their employer—all as a perk of employment.

To make it work that way, though, you need to know what your employees want and need. What workplace issues bother them? Maybe you can develop a campaign that addresses one or more of those issues. What social issues interest them? Develop a campaign that targets a common interest. By tailoring your campaign to employee concerns, you'll increase its effectiveness as a human resources tool.

To help you do this, ask the following questions:

1. What workplace issues are most pressing to employees?
2. What social issues are most pressing to employees?
3. Where do employees give time and money now?
   - To what organizations do they belong?
   - For what organizations do they volunteer?
4. Do we have an employee matching gift program? What organizations receive money?
5. Do we have an employee volunteer program?
   - Where do employees volunteer?
   - Do they enjoy this?
6. Are employees ever involved in "extracurricular" company events?
   - What kind of events?
   - Do employees enjoy these?
7. What skills do our employees have that would enable them to contribute effectively to a particular cause?

Community Affairs

If your company is at all involved in community issues, whether locally, regionally, or nationally, you may want to think about linking those goals to your campaign. Some companies have taken up the banner of education, for example, and have developed programs to strengthen local schools. Others have championed minority rights. Others have fought to keep a waste dump out of their town. Whatever the cause, you will be most effective if you pick one issue and put multiple corporate resources behind it. Working on several issues forces you to spread yourself too thin. If your partnership can be matched to an issue you are already tackling, so much the better.

1. With what issues is your company already involved?
   - environmental issues?
   - political issues?
   - economic issues?
   - cultural issues?
   - educational issues?
   - minority issues?
   - others?
2. Do any of these issues lend themselves to a partnership campaign?

Obviously, issues that are highly controversial don't make good marketing campaigns (unless you want to build your campaign on controversy). But education, the environment, minority and cultural issues, and many others are well suited for partnerships.

Business Development

Business development can include several types of activities: the development of new products or services, the development of new markets, or the development of new geographic territories. As you look ahead in your business, what new areas will you be moving into? A partnership campaign can be used to foster those efforts. It can be used to attract new customers, to help you position yourself with future partners, to develop goodwill in future market areas, and to build relationships that can lead to new products or services.

To help you keep your growth plans in mind as you weigh the possibilities for a campaign, ask yourselves the following questions:

1. What new market groups has the corporation decided to target?

2. Are there new product or service lines in development? For what markets?

3. What are the company's research and development needs? Are there universities or other types of nonprofits that might help?

Comparing Lists, Setting Goals

Once you've collected information from each department, you can use the data to develop goals for your partnership program. You'll try to develop a campaign that meets as many of those needs as possible. Start by having your team captain sum up each list on a separate sheet of paper; then call a meeting of the team. At the meeting, compare the lists. Are there any overlaps? Any target markets that show up on more than one list? Any social causes that repeat? Those are the areas that lend themselves most readily to a partnership campaign. As you discuss the lists, weighing the needs of different departments, the goals for the campaign will gradually become clear.

Image

Image is a big part of a partnership campaign, one of the major reasons for embarking on one. For your campaign to have the most impact, you need to be very clear about what image you want to project. That will determine what social cause you adopt, whom you pick as a partner, and how you design the campaign.

Your company may have already determined its corporate image, as well as that of individual products and services. You may have an advertising agency that has developed standards, slogans, and images to convey this image to the public. If so, review them. Do they mesh with the campaign goals and ideas you've generated? If so, how will you incorporate them into your plans? If not, how will you deal with the dissonance?

If you haven't already developed a clear corporate image, take some time now to do that. Did you list five words that describe your company when you were listing your marketing goals? If so, review them. Make sure everyone agrees. If not, do it now. Before you proceed with your campaign, you need to be able to define in five words, or one short sentence, the image it will convey.

Listing Possible Causes and Partners

As you compile your department lists, you may find that certain social causes or certain nonprofit organizations show up repeatedly. For instance, many employees may be interested in the same issue, and may support the same organization. Or employees may be interested in a social issue that is also relevant to your community affairs efforts. Or you may have given money to an organization that has several employees as members.

List all causes and organizations that show up on the lists. Mark any that occur more than once. These are natural causes and partners for you to consider as you develop a campaign.

Drafting a Public Purpose Partnership Philosophy

Now comes an important moment. As great as partnership is, your program can't be all things to all people. It can meet numerous corporate goals, but ultimately it will meet some better than others. Your job now is to decide which ones. You need to draft a partnership philosophy that will guide all your decisions from this point on.

• Will your program be primarily a marketing program? Will its first purpose be to increase sales, shelf space, inventory turnover, or other concrete measures of sales success? Will you design the program with those goals in mind? Will you expect it to perform like your conventional marketing programs? When you evaluate it afterward, will you be disappointed if it doesn't measure up to those expectations?

• Or will the program be primarily an image program? Will its main intent be to refine the way the public thinks of you? As you design the program, will you emphasize the image-building aspects and sacrifice, if necessary, sales inducements, or social gain, or employee benefits?

• Or will your program be primarily philanthropic? Will its first purpose be to do some good for a social cause? To give back to your community? To make the world a better place? Are you willing to sacrifice some profit for the cause?

• Or will your program be somewhere in between? Do you want to increase sales *and* help a worthy cause, realizing that each goal may bend a bit in service to the other?

• Why is your company doing this? Is it an appealing marketing technique that seems worth a try? Is it important to your image to appear socially responsible? Is your company genuinely committed to helping the community?

There are no right answers to these questions. What's important is that you talk about them *interdepartmentally;* that you hear how various members of the company think, learn what they expect; and that you come to a consensus. Your answers will be critical to the success of your program. They will determine how you design its elements; how you carry them out; and how you evaluate them afterward. If you can't agree now, you'll face unending conflict down the road—and few people will be happy with the outcome. But once you agree on the philosophy, you will be able to design a program that meets most people's needs; you'll be able to explain it convincingly to others; and you'll have solid ground for evaluating it once it's over.

WHICH GOALS ARE MOST IMPORTANT?

To help yourselves think through your partnership philosophy, try placing your expectations on the following grid. How does each member of your team expect the program to perform for each of the following goals? Use this as a starting point for your discussion.

Marketing (sales increases, traffic increases, etc.)	Image	Philanthropy (social good)	Human resources (employee benefit, recruitment, etc.)	Other (list)
High				
Medium				
Low				

CHAPTER 16

Picking a Cause

Fill in the blanks:

Possible Social Causes Our Company Could Adopt

1. My favorite causes:
   a. _____
   b. _____
   c. _____

Now that you've gotten that out of your system, we can go on.

The choice of social cause will be the single most important decision you make in your public purpose campaign. You want to make sure it's the right choice for your company—not just the right choice for you. That means you need to put more than personal preference into the decision: you need market research. You need to learn what social issues motivate your customers, potential customers, and employees. Then you'll know you've got a cause with charisma.

Market Research

To find out, ask each of those groups what turns them on, what troubles them, which issues they support, which issues they find a waste of time. Make your questions specific. Even within one issue, there are subgroups, and you want to home in as closely as possible on the issues that move your markets. Take the environment, for example. Within that one area you've got animal-lovers and tree-huggers; people fighting pollution and people building nature trails; people saving local wetlands and people saving the Amazon rain forests. Which cause appeals to your audience? What style of working? What geographic focus? For your campaign to be effective, you need to know the answers.

Ask each group which organizations they support. To what non-profits do they belong? To which do they send money? For whom do they volunteer? You'll come away with a gold mine of information about your markets' preferences—and a list of possible causes and partners for your partnership campaign.

Following Up the Research

More than likely, your research will turn up several causes that interest your several audiences. That means you've got some choices. Your task now is to narrow them down. Do that by asking yourselves two important questions:

1. Which issue is closest to our field of business?
2. Which issue can we own?

Close to Your Business

Picking an issue that's close to your business is extremely important for several reasons.

One, you want to create a logical fit in consumers' minds. People should say "Of course" when they hear what you're doing. That will help them remember. It will also make your efforts seem more credible.

Two, you want a cause on which you can have an impact. In an area related to your business, you already have contacts who can help you. Your employees are informed and motivated. Your business associates can be mobilized to participate. You've got a jump on the issue before you leave the gate.

Three, you want a cause that will motivate your customers. The closer the cause is to your business, the more persuasive it will be. Here's a good example. Ralston Purina has created a successful partnership campaign with the Humane Society featuring its lines of pet food. It is a classic cause-related marketing effort in which the company gives $.20 to the Humane Society for every pet food coupon redeemed, up to a ceiling of $1 million. The money goes to a program called Pets for People, which helps seniors adopt pets. Ralston was shrewd in adopting the Humane Society. As a pet food manufacturer, the company could have said, "We're in the animal care business." That would have opened up a broad list of causes to support: animal rights groups, animal welfare groups, save-the-animal groups. But Ralston didn't say that. Instead, it zeroed in much closer to its customer. The company said, "We're in the pet food business. We want to reach *pet owners*. What causes appeal to them?" Defining its business—and its customers—this narrowly led the company to the Humane Society's program. The resulting campaign has captured high visibility and approval with exactly the market Ralston want to reach.

Own Your Own

It is equally important to pick an issue you can own. As more and more companies get into public purpose marketing, it gets harder and harder to find a "new" issue. But try. Don't be a me-too player: be a leader. Pick an issue you can own; then stick with it. Your goal is to have an impact: to become identified with an issue and improve it. That's the way to build a reputation—not by spreading yourself too thin over a range of causes. The public won't remember if you've given a little to this cause, a little to that one, a little to the other.

Attention spans are too short. But the public will identify you with a cause if your partnership is long-term and effective.

How One Company Did It: Midland Bank

Midland Bank is one of Britain's largest financial institutions. In the spring of 1990 the bank decided to aggressively pursue public purpose partnering in order to strengthen its competitive position. Over the next several months, the bank systematically selected an issue to adopt. Here's how Midland made its choice.

Step 1: Establishing criteria for the cause. Midland's first step was to establish criteria a social issue must meet in order to be suitable for bank sponsorship. The bank decided on the following:

The issue must be:
- relevant and of interest to our customers and employees
- visible (i.e., the cause itself must be visible to the target markets, and the Bank's activity in that area must be visible)
- enduring
- complementary with the Bank's image as spelled out in our positioning statements: we are reliable, we are responsive, we are honest, we listen and we care, we look professional, we are a modern bank.

Step 2: Listing the possibilities. Midland broke the range of possibilities into six broad categories:

- sports
- arts
- environment
- education
- community
- health

Step 3: Evaluating the possibilities. Then the bank evaluated the possibilities in terms of the criteria it had established.

- Sports: "Sports is nearing its limits as a leisure time activity and there is near saturation of some sporting events in terms of sponsorship." Not enduring. Scratch it from the list.
- Arts: "Interest in the arts will continue to grow because of increasing leisure and the potential role of culture in the opening-up of Europe in 1992. Arts can include cinema, photography, pop and folk, as well as the more traditional classical music, opera and ballet. Sponsorship of the arts also offers corporate hospitality opportunities." Hmm. Relevant: yes. Visible: yes. Enduring: yes. Complementary: yes. A possibility.
- Education: "Education probably affords the least opportunities, not because it is not a relevant concern but because of the very fine line that educationalists draw between educating students/school children and advertising to them. It would be therefore difficult to exploit the promotional opportunities afforded by education." Complementary: no. Eliminate it.
- Environment: "Of the other issues, concern about the environment is a major area. After years of being regarded as a fringe issue, the environment, particularly global warming and the pollution of waters and rivers, has emerged as a key part of the political agenda. The growth in environmental issues will continue throughout the 1990s to a point where it is inextricably linked with daily political life, corporate strategy and the total marketing mix.

"However, whilst the environment is too important an area to ignore, the opportunities to strongly link our name with this issue are jeopardised by the rush of companies trying to own this area, a less good fit between banking and Green issues than, for example, between the Food Industry and the Green Lobby, and a growing cynicism on the part of consumers about some companies' real motives.

"Our approach to Green should be one of ensuring that the Bank satisfies the 'hygiene factors' rather than become a crusader for this cause." Relevant: yes. Visible: not very. Compatible: not really. Move on.

• Community: "The community, including urban renewal, has also emerged as a key issue. The last ten years of Thatcherism have seen a predominance of the 'private luxury/public squalor' attitude. However, more recently, individuals and businesses are being asked to adopt a sense of social responsibility and to reinvest income and profits for the common good.

"The breadth and depth of community issues, from inner city poverty to urban architecture, provide Midland with an enormous number of opportunities to involve and touch all sections of the community." Aha! Relevant: yes. Visible: yes. Enduring: yes. Complementary: yes. A distinct possibility.

• Health: "Health, whilst a very important issue, is not a useful issue for us in this regard because [in Britain] health is viewed as the responsibility of the government. It would be odd for a bank to adopt this issue when there are so many more immediate areas that need addressing." Relevant? yes. Complementary? No. Forget it.

Step 4: Ranking the issues. Midland then created a grid, ranking each of the issues in terms of its *relevance* to the bank's target audiences and the issue's overall *visibility*.

Step 5: Selecting the issue. Community wins! The rankings on the grid, combined with the broad range of partnership activities available, persuaded the bank to select the community as the focus of its campaign.

Having selected an issue, Midland is now working on a plan for developing partnership activities in its 1,500 branches. As this book goes to press, headquarters staff are surveying branch managers about local community issues, training branch personnel about the importance of responding to community concerns, and are deciding which aspects of the program should be controlled centrally and which at the regional and local levels. Midland expects to introduce its first partnership activities over the next several years.

MIDLAND BANK

Relevance and Visibility of Sponsorship Issues Amongst Major Target Groups

	Education		Environ.		Comm'y		Health		Arts	
	rel	vis	rel	vis	rel	vis	rel	vis	rel	vis
Personal Customers	7	2	9	3	8	9	6	7	4	2
Enterprise Customers	7	2	8	3	8	9	6	7	4	2
Corporate Customers	7	2	10	3	10	9	6	7	6	5
Opinion Formers	7	3	10	5	10	9	6	7	6	7
Staff	7	5	9	9	9	9	6	7	4	2

Key:
rel = relevance   10 = prime relevance/visibility
vis = visibility   1 = little relevance/visibility

CHAPTER 17

Picking a Nonprofit Partner

Compu-Sell, a chain of computer stores, is considering two nonprofit partners: The National Association for Missing Children (an agency that locates missing kids) and Second Helpings (a food bank). Which one should Compu-Sell pick?

If you said the National Association for Missing Children you have the same sense of logic as the general public—a highly desirable trait when it comes to public purpose marketing. The Association for Missing Children can use Compu-Sell's computers in its searches. That gives the chain a big hook to hang a marketing campaign on. It can advertise the number of kids who have been found thanks to the company's donation. Second Helpings, the food bank, is a great organization. It feeds a lot of people. But it won't beef up Compu-Sell's marketing goals because there's no logical connection between the chain's business and the food bank's.

A logical connection is critical not only when picking a social issue, but also when picking a partner. The right choice will attract the right audience and motivate it successfully. The wrong choice can turn people off, or worse, damage your reputation. How can you be sure to make the right choice? Measure each possible partner against the following criteria.

Pick a partner that matches your corporate image. Even within one issue, different nonprofits have different images. Consider Greenpeace and the Nature Conservancy: both work to protect the environment, but one is seen as radical, the other as conservative. As a result, they attract different clienteles and would reflect differently on corporate partners. You can use this fact strategically to help shape your company's image. For example, look at how partnering different arts groups or health-care agencies might reinforce your image:

- Do you want to be seen as strong, stable, and conservative? Pick a nonprofit with history and tradition; say, a fine arts museum, an orchestra, or an agency with a solid record in heart research.
- Do you want to be seen as adventuresome and pioneering? Partner a newer organization recognized for experimentation; say, a contemporary arts center, an experimental theater, or an organization that works for people with AIDS.
- Do you want to project an image of nurturing, warmth, and family values? Consider a children's museum, a zoo, or a children's hospital.

Each of these partners will help you attract a particular following, and each will project a certain personality. You'll be linking that personality to your own—so make sure it's the one your company wants.

Pick a partner that is credible in its field. Your partnership campaign will be only as strong as your nonprofit partner's reputation, so be sure you pick the best.

- Examine the nonprofit's track record. Has it had substantial accomplishments in its field?
- Examine its board. Is it governed by recognized experts?
- Examine its funding bases. Does it get grants from reputable sources?
- Examine its use of funds. Is the majority used for programs, not for fund-raising or administration?

Use experts in that area to help you pick a really solid partner. Don't rely on instinct; the people you're hoping to attract may know more about this organization than you do.

Pick a partner that is financially and operationally sound. You're not running a personality contest here; you're developing a business deal, and you need a partner you can depend on. To make sure you find one, examine the following:

- The organization's size and sophistication. Pick an agency that is well matched to your company. You want to look like partners—not like Mutt and Jeff.
- The organization's financial condition. Is it stable? Or will it need your venture to stay alive? Your partner may be saving a dying breed—but you don't want it to be one.
- The organization's operation. Is it businesslike? Are the staff strategic thinkers? Do they meet deadlines? Ask for references from others who have worked with the organization. You want a business partner, not a protégé.
- The organization's decision-making process. Is every decision a decision by committee? Can the organization develop systems for streamlining the process? Is the board involved in even minor decisions? This is potentially one of the trickiest areas in corporate-nonprofit partnerships. Flexibility on both sides will smooth the way considerably.

Pick a partner with a presence in the geographic areas you want to reach. People support causes that are close to home. Their loyalties are strongest to nonprofits in their own backyards. So when you pick a partner, pick one with a strong presence in the geographic areas you've targeted in your marketing plans.

- Are you creating a local marketing campaign? Pick a partner that targets the same area. It will give your campaign a hometown feel.
- Are you creating a regional campaign? Pick a nonprofit whose region corresponds to yours. Then work closely with it to tailor the campaign to regional interests.

- Are you creating a national campaign? Pick a nonprofit that operates nationally: it will reinforce your image across the country. But, if possible, work with the organization's chapters in different cities. Members and volunteers in those cities can be brought in to localize the campaign and give it a grass-roots character.

Pick a partner that will be yours exclusively. You want an exclusive on your issue. Likewise, you want an exclusive relationship with your nonprofit partner. Try to avoid organizations that have participated in campaigns with other companies. The public won't automatically associate them with you. It will be harder to forge a long-term partnership. And it will be harder for you to have a demonstrable impact on the issue. Instead, go for a nonprofit that's unattached. You'll be able to work with the organization to shape the campaign so that it meets your needs as well as the nonprofit's, without input from rival corporations.

Pick a partner you want to work with. Once you pick a partner, you're going to work with it for months or even years. Make sure you like it—its issue, its staff, the way they work and play. Make sure the staff like you. How do they feel about your business? Do they understand your needs? Or do they see you as a necessary evil on whom they must depend for needed funds? This project should be fun for both of you. Remember: you're going to hit hard times—when your cultures clash, when you don't see eye to eye. That happens on every project, not just in partnerships. But on most projects you don't get to pick your partners. Here you do. So do yourself a favor: pick one you like.

How One Company Did It: Scott Paper

In 1986, Scott Paper Company launched a line of paper products called Helping Hand. As described in Chapter 6, Helping Hand was designed as a permanent cause-related marketing effort, with a nickel of every purchase going to six charities that support children with special needs. To select the Helping Hand partners, Scott developed a list of partnership criteria. Each charity must:

1. have as its primary focus the Helping Hand priority of helping children with special needs.
2. have IRS status as a nonprofit, tax-exempt organization.
3. have a strong national presence and substantial size.
4. have strong public recognition and strong national support.
5. have a professional operation that is above reproach, with a long track record of success.
6. have a good reputation with the pediatric community.
7. have a strong local presence in communities across the country.
8. have a strong corps of volunteers who run its programs.
9. be actively interested in supporting the brand's success, and in building a mutually beneficial partnership.

Using these criteria, Scott selected as its Helping Hand partners the United Cerebral Palsy Society, Easter Seals, the March of Dimes, the National Association for Sickle Cell Disease, the Leukemia Society of America, and the Cystic Fibrosis Foundation.

Together they built a profitable brand with a distinctive image in the minds of consumers. The brand raised $3 million for the six charities and cemented Scott's corporate image as a company that cares about families.

How Not to Pick a Partner

Occasionally, you may want *not* to pick a partner. That is, you may decide that as part of your partnership strategy, you want to find a partner in an alternate way. For instance, you might want your customers to pick the partner. Or you might want a panel of experts to pick the partner. Or you might avoid a single choice and instead pick several partners. All of these choices are fine—as long as they are made strategically.

Letting Your Customers Pick the Partner

Remember MasterCard's "Choose to Make a Difference" Campaign in Chapter 6? This strategy worked very effectively for them, as it did for Ukrop's Supermarkets. The key to success here is to make the customer's choice the central element in the campaign.

If you want to use this approach:

1. Build your campaign around the fact that customers get to choose. Include that in all your campaign ads and literature. Make the customers' choice the selling point of the campaign.

2. In a local campaign with small donations, you can let your customers choose freely. However, in a regional or national campaign, or in a campaign with sizable donations, you should preselect a small number of recipient organizations. Otherwise, the number of choices made by customers will be unmanageable. Make sure your preselected choices meet all the criteria for partnership.

3. Publicize the results. In a local campaign with many recipients, publicize the list of recipients. Take out a full-page newspaper ad, or post the list in your store, or mail the list to your clients. It's important for people to know that their contributions were received and their voices were heard. In a regional or national campaign with preselected recipients, publicize the results of the customer "vote." Let customers know how much money they channeled to each organization so that they can feel good about their participation.

Letting a Panel of Experts Pick the Partner

American Express used this approach in a cause-related marketing campaign called Project Hometown America. AmEx wanted a campaign with a grass-roots personality. So it decided to contribute money to small organizations working in cities across America to improve their local communities. Rather than pick the many recipients itself, the company created a board of advisers made up of volunteers from organizations across the country. These people were qualified judges of local organizations, and better able to make the selections than the company would have been.

If you want to use this approach:

1. Make sure your panel is well qualified. Its members will reflect on your organization every bit as much as their choices, so they should also meet the criteria for public purpose partners.

2. Establish clear criteria for recipient organizations. Publicize those criteria so that customers know what types of organizations will be chosen.

3. Publicize the panel and its decision-making process. Make sure the process is straightforward and aboveboard.

4. Publicly celebrate the winners. Let people know where their money has gone.

Picking Several Partners

The danger in picking several partners is that it violates a very basic marketing rule: keep it simple. With multiple partners you run the risk of having your campaign appear unfocused. You also have more relationships to manage. If you decide to partner several non-profits, try the strategy Johnson & Johnson used in its "Shelter Aid" campaign (Chapter 6). The company had multiple nonprofit recipients but only one *cause*. In effect, the cause itself became the partner.

If you want to use this approach:

1. Pick nonprofits in a related field. You might pick three environmental organizations, four health-care organizations, or five arts organizations. But keep them all within a single cause.

2. Keep the overall number of nonprofits small. You want to have an impact on the issue. The fewer partners you have, the more money and help you will be able to give each one.

3. Make sure all the organizations meet your criteria for partners.

CHAPTER 18

Developing a Campaign

Nothing is more dangerous than an idea when it is the only one you have.

—Emile Chartier, French philosopher

You've set your goals. You've picked an issue. You've thought of partners. By this time, you've probably got a bunch of ideas for campaigns you'd like to launch. It's time to leap in, shake some hands, and sign some contracts, right? Wrong.

Before you approach a prospective partner, you need something to approach with: a package of solid venture ideas. You'll refine these ideas later, with your partner. But first you need to develop a package that works for you and that your partner can respond to. That means you need a campaign brainstorm. Why brainstorm new ideas when you already have several you like? For a number of reasons.

One, you want to avoid the trap of falling in love with your first idea. How do you know there isn't a better idea waiting to be discovered? Or a cluster of good ideas that you can carry out in combination? Unless you probe a bit, you'll never know what you're missing. You may well come back to the idea you started with. But if you do, you'll know for sure that it's the right one.

Two, you really want more than one idea. Your campaign will be strongest if it includes several separate, related ventures which can be rolled out in conjunction with each other. These will keep the program fresh in the public eye, give people numerous ways to get involved, and extend the program's life. Brainstorming will help you find a number of ideas you like, instead of just one or two.

Three, you need several good ideas with which to approach a nonprofit. The nonprofit's staff will want to feel that they can help shape the program, not that they're being offered a single idea, take it or leave it.

Four, ultimately you will work with your nonprofit partner to develop the campaign. The nonprofit will be an equal player in the venture, so the staff will get equal say in what you do. But if you spend time brainstorming ventures now, you'll go into those negotiations with a list of projects that meet your needs.

Five, brainstorming is fun. It's a freewheeling, no-holds-barred session in which you sit around a table, shouting, gesticulating, and interrupting each other while you think of all the ventures you could possibly do. Goofy ones. Serious ones. Great but impractical ones. Out of the mélange will come more solid ideas than you'll actually be able to use. So roll up your sleeves. Pour the coffee. And dig in.

The Brainstorm Session

Your brainstorm session should be attended by everyone on the core partnership team, as well as a few individuals chosen specifically for their creativity. These can be company insiders or complete strangers to the business. They can be people from your ad agency, if you have one and really like the way they think. The key requirement is that they be truly creative—that they be freethinkers who can take an idea and run with it. Keep the total number of brainstormers to ten or under.

We suggest that you hold the meeting in the morning when everyone is fresh. If possible, hold it *first thing* in the morning, before people have gone to their desks. You want them to be clear-headed, not distracted by today's concerns. Allow two hours—no more, no less. Two hours gives you enough time to warm up, get goofy, get serious, get ideas flowing, and then quit before you burn out.

A few days before the meeting, it's a good idea to circulate a two-page paper to all attendees explaining the reason for the meeting, the goals of the campaign, and the image words or slogan you've agreed on. Also include some background information on the social issue you've chosen and on your nonprofit partner, if you've picked one. A brochure from the partner would be best.

You should consider on the day of the meeting going into the conference room ahead of time with a pad of newsprint paper. Label each sheet with one of the partnership options described in Part II—cause-related marketing, premiums, sponsorships, licensing, sponsored ads, etc—and one sheet "other." Tack your sheets on the walls: you'll want to fill them with ideas before the meeting is through.

Designate one person—possibly the team captain—as the meeting's official facilitator and recorder. This person's job is to ask the questions, keep the meeting going, and take notes. The person you designate will have to be a good listener: he or she will do more writing than talking.

Start the meeting by going over the "givens"—the campaign goals, the social issue you've picked, your nonprofit partner, the image you want to project. Don't spend a lot of time; just make sure everyone's up to speed. Then, one by one, take up each of the campaign strategies listed on the walls around you. Ask yourselves: *What kind of cause-related marketing campaigns could we do that would meet our goals, work well with our prospective partner, and be fun and interesting to the public and the media? What kind of special events? What kind of premium items? What kind of sponsored ads?*

Take the strategies one at a time. Try to milk each one for all it's worth before going on to the next. The idea is to get as many ideas out as you can. Don't worry about quality. Quantity is what counts! Dumb ideas will lead to good ones. The point is to generate ideas that would never arise under more "orderly" circumstances.

When discussion starts to flag, move on to the next strategy. If an idea doesn't fit a strategy, put it on the sheet called "other." If the conversation takes you back to an earlier sheet, go with it. The goal is to leave the meeting having filled as much space on the walls as possible.

The process will start slowly, but by the end of two hours you should have generated a lot of heat, a lot of paper, and a lot of ideas. You'll have silly ones, impractical ones—but also a lot of good ones— ideas you never would have thought of had you stopped after your first few thoughts. Later you'll evaluate them all. For now, give yourselves a big pat on the back, sigh, and go back to your real jobs.

Post-Brainstorm Evaluation

Now that you've done the fun work, you need to do some serious work. You must evaluate all the ideas you came up with and decide which ones are worth pursuing. Some you'll discard immediately. Some will seem iffy. Some will seem downright doable. Narrow the list to ten or fewer and measure each of those against the following criteria.

1. **Goals:** Does this idea meet at least one, and preferably more, of your stated goals? If not, can it. You're not doing this campaign for brownie points. You're doing it for both corporate and social payback.

2. **Fit:** Is there a logical fit between this idea, your products and services, the social cause, and the nonprofit partner? If not, the public won't buy it.

3. **Simplicity:** Is the idea simple and easy to understand? Can you explain it in one sentence? Do people respond, "Gee, I wish I'd thought of that!"? If not, it's probably too complex and the public won't get it, either.

4. **Appeal:** Will it interest your target market? Do market research to test the idea. If it doesn't fly, forget it.

5. **Newsworthiness:** Will it attract specialty media that reach your target markets? Will mass media pick it up? Test the

idea on friends in the media to see if they like it as much as you do.

6. **Longevity:** Will it sustain the public's interest for as long as it needs to? Or will it get old before its time?

7. **Ownership:** Will your company be able to "own" the program in the public's mind? If you can't get an exclusive—at least in your own industry—rethink the program, the cause, and the partner.

8. **Merchandising potential:** Are there merchandising opportunities attached to this idea? Can you create point-of-purchase displays? Discount coupons? In-store events? Souvenir products? What additional revenue generators can be attached to the campaign?

9. **Cost-effectiveness:** Is this a good use of your dollars? Or would you get as much return by spending them in a different way?

10. **Employee appeal:** Will your employees respond to it? Is there room for them to participate?

11. **Middleman support:** Will retailers, distributors, salespeople, and anyone else you depend on to get your products or services to the public respond to it? You may be counting on them for support.

12. **Management support:** Will management get behind it in a big way? If not, better not do it.

Any venture idea that passes this test packs a lot of potential.

How One Company Does It: Payless Cashways

Payless Cashways, a national retailer of lumber and home-improvement products with headquarters in Kansas City, has done numerous public purpose partnerships. Over the years, Payless has developed the following criteria for evaluating possible ventures.

1. The theme of the venture should:
   - be "warm and fuzzy" and appeal to customers' altruism.
   - be simple, distinctive, and easy to grasp.
   - appeal to as wide an audience as possible.
   - promote our marketing message.
   - strengthen our image as good public citizens.
   - be related to our line of business, if possible.

2. The venture should promote sales and/or build traffic to our business.

3. The venture should appeal to employees. It should offer them a way to be involved and, if possible, control elements of it.

4. The venture should be easy to operate. It should be managed by the nonprofit (or an outside contractor) and should require little time from corporate staff.

5. If the venture starts locally, it should have regional and/or national roll-out potential.

6. The venture should be easy to explain and defend to shareholders.

7. The venture should be newsworthy and appealing to the media.

8. The venture should be compatible with our corporate giving guidelines.

9. The venture should be low-risk.

10. The venture could have a seasonal focus.

11. We should have exclusive rights to the program.

12. The venture should encourage the nonprofit's members and users to participate.

13. The structure of the venture should allow for corporate review at predetermined checkpoints.

CHAPTER 19

Piggyback Ventures

A fool who persists in his folly becomes wise.

Once you've evaluated each idea, you'll have a short list of projects with big potential. Your next task is to think about how to turn those ideas into a campaign. You have two options. One is to pick out your favorite and run with it: you can do a one-shot event, hope it's a big success, then think about venture number two. Good plan. Your second option is to do "piggyback ventures," a multilayered campaign in which you and your nonprofit partner enter into several ventures together, rolling one out after another, over a longer period. This is an even better plan, although there are pros and cons to both arrangements.

The One-Shot Campaign

The main advantage of a one-shot campaign is that it's easy. You and your nonprofit partner agree on a venture you would like to pursue, you implement the campaign, and you're done. At that point you can sit back, evaluate the results, and decide whether you want to do more. No muss. No fuss. No long-term commitment. If you had a difficult working relationship, if partnerships don't suit you, you can exit gracefully.

One-shot campaigns are an excellent way to get started in partnering. They give both partners a chance to test the waters, learn about each other, learn about the process, and then decide whether and how to proceed. They are definitely recommended for beginners.

The disadvantage of one-shot campaigns is that they don't take maximum advantage of a corporate-nonprofit partnership. You've gone to the trouble of picking a cause, building a relationship, positioning yourself in the public mind—and then it's all over in a flash. There's no continuing public reminder. No continuing consumer interaction. No continuing glory. A far more effective way to build a partnership campaign is to design it for a longer term. That produces greater gain for the corporation, for the nonprofit, and for the cause.

Advantages of Piggyback Ventures

In a piggyback, or multilayered, campaign, the corporation and the nonprofit plan a *package* of ventures. Each venture is related to the others and rolls out according to a preset timeline. Each venture reinforces the others, and each offers the public a different way to get involved.

There are numerous advantages to this arrangement.

1. **Ownership:** A piggybacked campaign cements your partnership in the public mind. The variety of events and continuing nature of the campaign constantly remind the public that you are working together.

2. **Longevity:** A piggybacked campaign can keep the partnership in the public eye for an extended period. But with new events constantly emerging, it remains continually fresh.

3. **Commitment:** By building a long-term, many-pronged relationship with the nonprofit, you affirm your company's commitment to its cause. Your actions say *We genuinely care about this issue; we're not just here to make a buck.*

4. **Continuing benefit:** A piggybacked campaign enables you to benefit from continuing progress in your adopted cause. For instance, if a breakthrough is made in medical research that your campaign helped fund, you'll still be in the limelight when the breakthrough happens. If your campaign raises money for a new building for your partner, you'll still be there to bask in the glory when the building opens.

5. **Maximum impact:** A piggybacked campaign produces maximum gain for your partner and allows you to have maximum impact on the cause. Because your partner is showcased repeatedly to the public, it has many chances to broadcast its message; consumers have many chances to learn about the organization and get involved. And in a piggybacked campaign, you can offer more than money to the cause. You can use your employees to lend manpower. You can use your contacts with decision-makers to influence policies. You can give in-kind donations of equipment you no longer need. Each new offering can become a new element in your campaign, giving you numerous ways to keep the campaign fresh without spending more money.

6. **Maximum impact, period:** Targeting one issue with a variety of corporate resources will have much more impact on the issue—and on the public—than spreading your resources over several issues. A piggybacked campaign is the best way to do that.

Of course, there's a down side to all this. A piggybacked campaign is more expensive to produce than a one-shot deal. The timing and coordination are more complex. It takes time and effort to keep the elements running smoothly. And it requires a good working relationship between the partners. But those things are manageable—and often get easier as a campaign unfolds.

For that reason, we recommend that you develop a package of ventures that can be combined into a piggybacked campaign—but that you execute only the first. After it's over, sit back and evaluate it.

Did it do what you wanted? Did you like your partner? If yes, you're on a roll; bring out the rest of the package. If not, shake hands and say good-bye. You can try again in the future.

Time Frame

As you plan your piggybacked campaign you'll need to determine several things: the life span of each individual event, the spacing of the events, and the duration of the entire campaign.

Individual Events

Individual events tend to suggest their own duration. A special event such as a concert may last only two hours, with attendant promotion stretching out to a month. A cause-related marketing campaign may last three months. Most events have a natural life span which you should respect. However, keep in mind as you plan that short-term events may cost almost as much as medium- or long-term events, but give the public a much shorter time to respond. By the same token, events that last longer than three months may get stale as their novelty wears off.

Event Spacing

When you plan the spacing of individual events within a piggy-backed campaign, think about the pacing of the overall campaign. You may want some events to roll out rapidly to build impact. Others may happen slowly, with a lag of as much as six months in between. Your goal is to maintain an element of surprise: the public should never know what's coming next—or when it will come. As you plot a timeline for the campaign keep in mind the public's attention span, internal events in both organizations that may affect your ability to implement the campaign, and events in the outside world with which you may want to affiliate, or which you may want to avoid.

Campaign Duration

How long should a piggybacked campaign last? It depends—on the relationship between the partners, on the urgency of the cause, on the receptivity of the public. Numerous factors determine the best length for a campaign. Potentially a campaign can last for years. As mentioned earlier, Texaco has partnered the Metropolitan Opera since 1940. Procter & Gamble has partnered the Special Olympics since 1981. As long as the partnership continues to satisfy both partners, why not keep it going? The important thing is to evaluate it regularly in order to know how well it's performing. Here are some things to look for.

• **Effectiveness:** Is the campaign working? Is it producing the results you anticipated? If not, there's not much point in keeping it around, unless you can fix it to get the results you want. See Chapter 24, "Evaluating Your Campaign," for tips on determining its effectiveness.

• **Public perception:** Is the public still excited? Don't let the campaign overstay its welcome. Everything gets tired after a while, so you want to be on the lookout for early-warning signs of campaign fatigue. It's better to end a campaign early while public enthusiasm is still high than hang on too long. You can always bring it back later: people will be delighted to see an old friend return. But an event that has overstayed will be dead for all time. Use market research throughout the campaign to stay in touch with public perception. That way you'll always know what to do. (In your research, be sure to distinguish between the entire piggybacked campaign and individual campaign elements. The public may grow tired of a single element without tiring of the entire campaign.)

• **Partner satisfaction:** Are you still enjoying the campaign? Is your partner? If dissatisfactions are overtaking benefits, it's time to call a halt. Your campaign management will suffer if you're not having fun. Find an issue and a partner you'll enjoy.

• **Issue urgency:** Is the issue still pressing? Very occasionally, social issues disappear because major strides are made. If that happens on your issue, great! Declare victory and move to a new cause.

But don't expect it to happen. Most issues are ineradicable. Your goal should be to adopt an issue for the long term and really make a difference. Be wary of being faddish. If you move from one issue to another, constantly looking for the most popular cause, you'll be branded insincere.

Test-Market Your Campaign

Most companies test-market a new product before rolling it out in a full-scale launch. If you're planning a national partnership campaign, consider test marketing it, too. Testing lets you gauge the public's interest. Equally important, it enables you to work out the bugs before going national. Pick one city for your trial. Work closely with your retailers, salespeople, or other "middlemen" and with your partner's local chapter (if it has one) to plan and execute each element. Then evaluate carefully. You'll gain important information that can influence the rest of the campaign.

First Brands, manufacturer of Glad Bags, has done a multiyear campaign with Keep America Beautiful (KAB). Called the Glad Bag-a-Thon, the campaign was introduced in 1985 to highlight Glad's new Handle-tie trash bag. The idea behind the campaign was that citizens in local communities would take a day to clean up their city, using, of course, Glad Handle-tie bags. To test the idea, Glad partnered five KAB chapters in five cities. That gave Glad a chance to learn how to work with the organization and how to organize an event that depended quite literally on the kindness of strangers. The following year the company took the campaign national.

CHAPTER 20

More than Money

We think we can bring our expertise in advertising and promotion to bear in helping to achieve broader societal goals.

—Robert M. Viney, associate advertising manager with responsibility for environmental marketing policy, Procter & Gamble

Money may make the world go around, but to a nonprofit many other things can be almost as helpful. As mentioned earlier, corporations have a wealth of nonmonetary assets that can be valuable to a non-profit partner. Lending or donating those items can extend your campaign, giving it longer life in the public eye. In Part II we examined the variety of in-kind donations a company can make. This chapter will help you locate donate-ables within your company, and suggest ways to incorporate them into a campaign.

Employee Volunteers

As mentioned earlier, encouraging your employees to volunteer for your partner creates a win-win-win situation. The nonprofit gets needed manpower, as well as valuable skills it may be missing. The employee gets a chance to contribute directly to a social cause and to develop skills he or she may not use at work. The company benefits from the employee's development and improved morale.

Volunteering can happen at either the management or employee level. Employees provide much-needed manpower to a nonprofit. They are especially valuable if they volunteer regularly and get to know the organization. Managers can be equally valuable because they can be loaned for their specific skills. Does your partner need help with accounting? Lend someone in your business office for two hours a week who can help strengthen the system. Does your partner need help with marketing? Put your marketing manager on call for ten hours a month to help develop a marketing plan.

To implement this, you could circulate a survey asking employees about their volunteering preferences. What kinds of agencies would they like to work for? What kind of work would they like to do? How much time could they spend? What skills do they have that they would like to use in a volunteer capacity?

In-Kind Donations

As we said in Chapter 13, things that you take for granted may be extremely valuable to your nonprofit partner. In casting about for possible in-kind donations, ask yourselves three questions:

1. *What are we throwing away?*
Are you redoing your offices? Installing new equipment? Discarding reject product? Ask whether your partner can use your throwaways. Many a nonprofit is furnished, equipped, or fed with corporate discards.

2. *What services do we perform in-house that we could also perform for our partner?*

Do your in-house facilities sometimes have down time? Would your employees enjoy tackling a new and different project? Find out whether your partner can use those services. Possibilities include printing facilities, delivery and transportation facilities, warehousing facilities, photographic or videotaping services, art direction or production services, copywriting services, data processing services, and research services.

3. *Can our partner use our commercial product or service?*

Is the product or service you sell something your partner can use? Do you have overstock? Seconds? Products that have been replaced by newer versions? Companies that donate current inventory to nonprofits are eligible for a "stepped up" tax donation. Companies that donate services can take tax deductions for out-of-pocket expenses.

Consider using a clearinghouse, such as Gifts in Kind America in Alexandria, Virginia, or the National Association for the Exchange of Industrial Resources (NAEIR) in Galesburg, Illinois. They can arrange single donations or develop a turnkey giving program for you.

Facility Use

Does your company have facilities it doesn't use all the time that might be useful to your nonprofit partner? Possibilities include vans, office space, conference rooms, and warehouses. A real estate developer in New York City found that the recession was reducing the demand for condominiums in his buildings, so he began offering the empty spaces to local nonprofits, which used them for additional office space. An equipment repair shop next door to a small museum didn't need all its workshop and warehouse space, so it loaned part of the space to the museum, which installed its own carpentry shop. These types of loans save nonprofits thousands of dollars a year in facility costs.

Clout

One of the most helpful things you may be able to give your non-profit partner is clout; that is, your corporate weight applied to its cause. Most nonprofits work hard to effect change in a particular area, but they often lack the contacts or "pull" with officials that can readily promote change. As a business, you may be better positioned to get legislators, other businesses, or community leaders to take action. This works in your interest as well, since once you have adopted a cause, any improvement in that area reflects well on you. As Peter B. Goldberg, former head of the Primerica (Corporation) Foundation, said in talking about how business can further a social agenda, "A corporation can't simply put its money where its mouth is; it's got to put its mouth in the corridors of local, state, and federal governments."

As one part of its Social Responsibility Marketing partnerships program, for example, Easter Seals recruits high-level officers from its corporate partners to sit on its national and local boards. These individuals agree to hire more disabled workers in their businesses, and agree to act as advocates at the community level for disabled children. The clout and example of these corporate leaders add significantly to the impact of Easter Seals' message.

Marketing and Promotion

Your marketing skill is one of the most valuable things you can offer a nonprofit. As we said earlier, the nonprofit's goal is to get its message out to the public—both to educate the public and to attract new donors. Since most nonprofits are not experienced marketers, your professional help is extremely valuable.

- Give your nonprofit partner access to your in-house marketing, promotion, and advertising staffs, as well as to your external contractors. Use those people to work on your partner's programs: the better your partner looks, the better you look.

- Involve your partner in developing the promotional aspects of your campaign so that it learns from the experience.
- Include information about your partner in your billing statements or other literature. Mention it in your ads. This cements your relationship in the public mind, and it helps your partner get its message out.

Scott Paper Company offered this kind of assistance to the six charities that received proceeds from the Helping Hand product line. The charities believed this was one of the most beneficial parts of the partnership, since it provided continuing benefit after the campaign itself had ended. "Marketing professionals can provide technical assistance that could have a lasting impact on charitable organizations," said Cynthia Giroud, formerly Manager of Corporate Social Investment for Scott Paper. "This was one of the major benefits identified by the Helping Hand charities. Working with our advertising agency and marketing group gave them insight into the planning process, the analysis needed for program development, and ways to evaluate the results of their efforts."

Purchasing Goods or Services

You probably purchase a wide range of products and services from a wide range of vendors. Consider adding your partner to your vendor list. For example:

- If you partner a social service agency: can it offer classes or services for your employees on issues related to its mission, such as crime prevention, substance abuse, or other topics of employee concern?
- If you partner a health agency: can it offer classes or information packets for employees on topics such as weight loss, smoking cessation, stress reduction, or other areas of employee concern?

• If you partner a school, university, or job training program: can you use its students or trainees as interns?

• If you partner an arts organization: can you buy bulk tickets at discount prices to give to employees as perks?

Think creatively about your partner's business—and about your own needs. You may find more overlap than you first assumed.

Giving Money

Of course, if in addition to all these nonmonetary ways to help, you still want to give a nonprofit money—well, not many will refuse. Here are three things you might consider, in addition to a straight donation:

• Low-interest or no-interest loan: loan the organization money at low or no interest. Take a tax deduction for the interest you're not charging. If the loan is not paid back, it will become a tax-deductible contribution.

• Employee matching gifts: you'll increase the impact of your donations *and* please your employees if you offer to match their gifts to nonprofit organizations. This will also be a good way for you to keep tabs on the groups your employees are supporting so that you can be sure to keep your partnership campaign close to their hearts.

• Link your charitable giving program to organizations in which your employees volunteer. Many companies give small grants to any nonprofit for which an employee works regularly for six months or longer.

Incorporating Gifts into Your Campaign

Each of these gifts to a nonprofit partner can become an element in your campaign. Each one can be staged as a media event, designed to call attention to your gift and to keep your partnership in the public eye. In this way they can be used to extend your campaign and keep it fresh.

That doesn't mean that each gift should become a hollow play for publicity—not at all. The insincerity would show and the campaign would backfire. The donations should be genuine responses to needs of the nonprofit, and integral parts of your continuing campaign. They should be indications of your company's continuing commitment to this cause.

To use donations as part of your campaign, first think about what you have to give. Talk to people in different departments to see what corporate resources are being underused. Make a list of possible donations. Then talk to your partner: ask what it needs, and see if together you can expand the list.

Once you've settled on a list of donations, think about how you want to present each one to get maximum benefit for the cause and for yourself. For instance, if you decide to launch an employee volunteer program, can you launch it with a flourish? Perhaps by staging a media event on the first day of volunteering? Or by inviting the press to view the visible results of the first 100 hours of your employees' time? Not only will the nonprofit benefit from coverage on the evening news, but your employees will feel proud. This may help encourage additional employees to volunteer.

As you plan your campaign to include both marketing events and donation elements, think about the level of "flash" you want each element to have. Some—particularly the marketing events—can be "noisy," full of hype and excitement. Others—particularly the donations—can be "quieter," using feature stories rather than ad campaigns. Some stories can be targeted to special-interest media, others to mass-market outlets. Think about using donations as "spacers" between your marketing events to vary the "pitch" of your campaign and keep the public interested. For instance, after conducting a cause-related marketing campaign that lasts for three months, do some behind-the-scenes giving. Then six months later tell the public what you've been doing, or let it see the results.

By mixing marketing events with donations, you cement your relationship with the nonprofit, maximize your ability to make a difference for its cause, and remind the public of just how committed you are. After all, consumers are buying into your campaign because they support your partner. They want to know that you really support that partner, too. The more ways you can show them, the better.

CHAPTER 21

Telling the Public What You're Doing

If you did it and you didn't tell anybody, . . . you didn't do it.

—Bette Fenton, vice president for community relations
and public affairs, B. Dalton Booksellers

Planning a Comprehensive Publicity Campaign

Let's be honest. You do public purpose partnerships because you want to make a difference. You want to contribute to a worthy cause. You want your employees to feel proud. *And you want the world to know.* If the world doesn't know—if you don't broadcast your campaign message loud and clear—you'll miss out on a lot of the benefits that can come from your good works. To get those benefits, you need to plan a strategic publicity campaign that will get you the kind of attention you want. This will be a little different from planning your conventional promotional campaign because with a public purpose partnership there are more angles open to you, and you want to take them all.

To craft your public relations plan, work with your nonprofit partner. Your partner's input will be critical because it will have ideas and contacts that you won't have. If you have a PR firm you like, invite its staff, too. Together you can explore the wide variety of avenues open to unusual partnerships like yours.

Getting the Broadest Coverage

Because you are working with a nonprofit on a social issue, you'll have a wider range of media outlets available to you than you ordinarily would. Be systematic in pursuing them so that you get the widest— or most targeted—coverage possible.

1. Think about mass-market media: what newspapers, magazines, radio programs, and TV programs might be interested in your campaign? The list will be longer than the one you're used to because of the nature of the campaign. What publications do your target markets read? What do your partner's members read? Read those publications to get a feel for their stories, then think about how you can turn your campaign into a story that will interest them.

2. Think about targeted media: are there special-interest magazines, newsletters, or newspapers that might be interested? What about cable TV stations? What special-interest magazines or television programs do your target markets follow? Your partner's members? How can you make your campaign of interest to them?

3. Use all your partner's nonprofit communication channels: does it have a newsletter or magazine? Place a story there. Does it belong to a nonprofit association that has a newsletter or magazine? Plant a story there. Does it have media contacts who like the organization and are likely to take a story? Have your partner contact those reporters. In general, you are better off having the nonprofit place the stories because it will have more credibility than you will.

4. Use fully all your own communication outlets as well as those of your industry. These include your own newsletters or magazines, your billing statements or inserts, industry trade papers, etc.

5. Develop public service announcements. A PSA, whether print

or broadcast, can be designed to look and feel and draw like any other ad. However, there are restrictions on its placement and content. PSA's must be placed by the nonprofit. They are aired at the discretion of the television station; you can't control the air time. And they can advertise only the nonprofit activity. Your company can be mentioned as a sponsor of the program, but the PSA can't be an ad for your company, or even for your campaign. For example, if you are partnering a nonprofit in a special event, the PSA can advertise the event, mentioning you as a sponsor. It can't mention your product. Despite these restrictions, PSA's are an excellent way to generate free publicity that benefits your partner and links your name with its name.

Finding New Angles on the Story

Working with a nonprofit also means you have more stories to tell, and more ways to tell them, than you ordinarily would. You may be accustomed to using ads as your primary means of communicating with the public, but in this campaign you can use hard news stories, feature stories, PSA's, *and* straight ads. You can also tell your campaign story more than one way—to get the greatest amount of coverage. Here are some tips to guide you through story creation and placement:

1. Think about which aspects of your partnership are best suited to news stories and which are better promoted through advertising. You want a blend of hard news, feature stories, and ads. Plan a campaign that includes all three.

2. Look for topical issues you can relate your campaign to. Has a survey been released on a subject related to your cause? Has there been a scientific breakthrough in a related area? Has some news story appeared that calls attention to the issue? Use those events as opportunities to plant a story.

3. Do the same with holidays and special recognition periods. Is there a Christmas angle to your campaign? A Mother's Day connection? A special recognition period which your partner will

know about? Consider any external events relevant to your cause as possible media opportunities.

4. Look at your story from the point of view of the media person you are pitching. What will make this story interesting to him or her? Paint the story in that light. You ought to be able to sell the same story to *Sports Illustrated* and *Modern Maturity* just by refocusing the lens through which you see it.

5. Don't make your company the focus of the story. That will appear self-serving and will turn off most media. Instead, look for the angle of the story that will appeal to that magazine's readers or that program's viewers.

6. Remember: you don't need to reach everyone in America or everyone in your community. You need only reach the people you and your partner have targeted as your likely customers and supporters. Your audience may be in the millions—or it may be as few as ten thousand, depending on how you define the target group. Whatever its size, your goal is to reach those people in as many ways as possible, through a variety of media, so that they will hear your message and respond.

Being Clear

It's easy in conducting a media campaign to get caught up in hype. You're excited about what you're doing and you want your excitement to show. But there is a point at which hype turns into dishonesty. Steer clear of it. Don't exaggerate to the public about what the campaign will achieve. Don't suggest a relationship with the nonprofit that doesn't exist. Don't overstep the bounds of common sense and good taste. Doing those things will discredit your partnership—and your reputation along with it. To avoid problems, follow these guidelines as you plan your media campaign:

1. Be clear with your partner *ahead of time and in writing* about what is allowable and what isn't.

- What restrictions apply to using your partner's name and logo? When can it use yours?

- What information will be included about the organization? Name, address, and phone number? Information about the cause? Information about becoming a member or making a donation? Will this be in all campaign promotion or only in selected ads and stories?
- Will partners talk to reporters together or can each partner give interviews alone?
- Do both partners have veto power over ads and PSA's?
- Will your product names appear in campaign materials?
- How will you describe the campaign to the public? Agree on wording ahead of time.

Work together to develop and implement the publicity campaign. Your partner needs the experience of participating in a promotional campaign. You need your partner's credibility in contacting the media. You both need open and frequent communication to avoid misunderstandings and bad feelings.

2. Be clear with the public about how the money will be raised and allocated. The public will support your campaign because it believes in the cause. Your supporters will want to know exactly how your partner will benefit.

- Be clear about any limitations on your gift to the nonprofit. Is there a ceiling on your donation? What is it?
- Be honest. Do public purchases really trigger the donation, or will you make the donation regardless? Don't make it look like cause-related marketing if it's really a philanthropic gift. You're doing this program to strengthen your reputation; that reputation depends on honesty.
- Be forthcoming about the results. The public wants to know how well the campaign did. Did it achieve the projected results? How much money did the nonprofit get? How will it use that money? Several months later, take out ads that tell the public how your partner used the funds. It will be one more chance to remind consumers about how you contributed to the cause.

The Golden Rule

Include your partner in your ads. A nonprofit can't afford to buy the ad space you can. So one of the best ways you can help is by including your partner's message in your ads. Your partner gets its message broadcast. You look like a million dollars.

Communicating the Results

In all the excitement of creating your campaign, don't forget to communicate the results. A common tendency is to put so much effort into the front end of the program that you forget completely about the back end. But that's a bad tendency for a number of reasons:

1. Customers want results. The customers who supported your campaign want to know what it achieved. If they gave money, where did their money go? How was it used? How much was collected altogether? If you make them feel as if they genuinely helped the cause, they'll be much more likely to participate again next time. Customers also want to know that you did what you said you would. They supported you on faith, in the belief that you would help a cause they cared about. Afterward they want to know that you delivered, so that they know they made a good decision.

2. Employees want results. Your employees were involved in this campaign and they want to know what their efforts accomplished. Even employees who were not actively involved want to know that their employer is really making a difference. The campaign's achievements will make them feel proud.

3. You want results. You want to be able to say, *Look what a difference we made on this issue!* Being able to publicize the results is one of the best reasons to do a partnership. Don't write off that opportunity!

4. Publicizing results extends your campaign. It offers you one

more opportunity to grab the spotlight and remind the world about your partnership.

5. Publicizing results benefits your partner. It gives your partner a chance to showcase its accomplishments, and the more accomplished it is, the better able it will be to attract donations.

What Do We Mean By Results?

When we say publicize results we don't just mean the amount of money collected during your campaign. That's nice. The public wants to know about it. But there should be other results as well. For instance, as a result of your campaign:

- how many new donors does your partner have?
- how many new volunteers?
- how many more people has it fed? (Or how many more plays has it produced, or how many more people with AIDS has it cared for?)
- what legislation has been proposed to improve the issue?
- what progress has been made on the cause?

Dollars are nice—but abstract in this context. The public wants to help make a difference. It wants to know about tangible results it helped create. That strengthens its connection with the cause and, therefore, with you.

If you're building a continuing campaign with your partner, create milestones ahead of time, then advertise each time you reach one: the one hundredth new volunteer, the one thousandth adult who learned to read, the first patient to receive a new treatment. Each of these becomes one more way to extend your campaign, and one more way for the public to know that, together, you're making a difference.

One Last Piece of Advice

Forgive us. This will sound obvious. Hardly worth saying. But you'd be surprised how necessary it is. **Don't forget to publicize your campaign.**

Why did we have to say that? Especially at the end of a chapter about publicity? Because you wouldn't believe the number of businesses that do public purpose partnering and don't tell anyone they're doing it. We know of ten businesses—no exaggeration—in Seattle that are conducting public purpose partnership campaigns that nobody knows about. A supermarket chain that gives $.10 to the Nature Conservancy every time a customer brings his or her own shopping bag. A coffee retailer that gives $4 to CARE every time someone buys a gift pack of coffee beans. Restaurants that give a portion of every meal to local food banks. But you walk into any of these establishments and there's no sign in the place describing their donation. There's no mention in any of their ads. Even the salespeople don't always tell you.

Why? We're not sure. Perhaps they feel they are conducting these campaigns out of the goodness of their hearts, purely for the benefit of the nonprofit with no gain for themselves. That's fine! But would their partners benefit any less if consumers knew the campaigns were happening? Of course not! If anything, they would benefit more because consumers would patronize the businesses to support those organizations. The businesses are also missing an opportunity to educate the public about their partners. If the coffee company really wants to benefit CARE, shouldn't it put information about the organization in its store? Or in its ads? Or on its bags? We suspect the real reason these companies don't publicize their campaigns is simply that they've neglected to.

So, please: be as selfless, as noncommercial, as low-key as you like in conducting your campaign. But don't be neglectful. If you don't want to attract money and attention to yourself—at least get them for your nonprofit partner. After all, isn't that why you're doing this?

CHAPTER 22

Getting Employees on Board

"I would now like you to tell me to what extent you agree or disagree with each statement I read out.

"A company that supports society is probably a good company to work for."

Strongly agree	29%
Tend to agree	57%
Neither agree nor disagree	9%
Tend to disagree	3%
Strongly disagree	*
Don't know	2%

—Survey by Mori, a British market research firm, 1990

One of the biggest reasons to embark on a partnership campaign is to boost employee morale. That means employees should be involved in shaping and implementing the campaign from the beginning. You want them to feel some ownership of the program, not that it is a fait accompli handed down from above. Work with your human resources people to plan employee involvement. Let them tell you how to design the campaign to best meet employee needs.

Maximizing Employee Satisfaction

1. Communicate strategically. As you plan your communications package, don't forget your employees. Think of them as an audience to be communicated with the same way you think about your external markets. Plan a communications campaign for them, the same way you do for the media.

2. Use multiple media. Use a variety of media to tell employees about the campaign: in-house newsletters, bulletin boards, staff meetings—whatever vehicles you generally use for communicating with workers. The more you talk to them about the campaign the more seriously they will take it.

3. Start early. Don't wait until you launch your campaign to tell your employees you're doing it. Include them in the decision. They'll know you're thinking about it because, presumably, you've asked them about causes and nonprofits they support. Tell them the results of your market research. As you narrow the field to a few causes and a few nonprofits, ask them their opinions. If you keep them involved throughout the process, they'll feel greater ownership once the campaign is announced.

4. Keep them informed. Before you launch any aspect of the campaign, and before you leak any news to the press, be sure your employees know about it. Don't set them up to be surprised when events or stories break. They should feel like insiders—after all, this is their campaign, too. And, you don't want them to be embarrassed if a customer or a friend asks them about the campaign and they don't know anything about it. Your employees are ambassadors between you and the outside world. Make sure they are well briefed.

5. Solicit employee input. Create two-way channels for communicating about the campaign: perhaps an employee newsletter to which they can write letters, a bulletin board (electronic or otherwise) on which they can post suggestions, or even a suggestion box. Appoint an "answer person" for the campaign—someone employees can go to with comments or questions. Then take their comments seriously. Revise the campaign from time to time in response to their suggestions; then let them know you have done so. The more ownership they feel, the more benefit you will derive.

6. Showcase employee involvement. As employees get involved in the campaign—whether through volunteering, donating, or working on the campaign itself—place stories about their involvement in both in-house and external media. The publicity will make them proud and will encourage others to get involved, too.

7. Be clear. Make the terms of employee involvement clear. Is it mandatory? Does it have an impact on evaluations? Will employees be penalized for not participating? One hopes that the answer to all these questions is no—but employees may not know that. Make it clear.

8. Showcase management support. Support for your campaign must start at the top, and employees need to know it's there. Have top executives address staff meetings. Have them write stories in the newsletter. Have them volunteer for the nonprofit to set an example. Use whatever means work in your corporate culture to let management express its belief in the program. Employees want to know that the program is heartfelt and long-term. It will be hard for them to take it seriously if they think the big guns don't care.

Involving Your "Middlemen"

All the rules that apply to involving employees apply equally to involving "middlemen"—your sales force, your franchises, your distributors, anyone you count on to get your product or service to the public. These people can often make or break a campaign by lending or withholding their support. Make sure they like the campaign! Get them involved at the beginning.

1. Do market research. When you poll your customers and employees about what causes and nonprofits they support, poll your middlemen, too.

2. Keep in touch. Use a campaign newsletter or other vehicle to communicate with them regularly. Give them the big picture of the campaign so they know what to expect when; then give them regular updates to let them know what's happening. Include stories *from* middlemen in your communications. They're close to the action, so they should have good stories. And you'll be recognizing their involvement.

3. Solicit their input. Appoint someone to be the communications link with these people and make sure that person solicits input on a regular basis. Your middlemen are a lot closer to the action than you are in your corporate offices. They also know their territories better than you do. Give them a hand in shaping the program so that it will work on their turf; then solicit and respond to their feedback once the campaign is in action.

4. Emphasize home team support. Make it clear that the home office is serious about the program. It will be tough for your middlemen to get behind it if it seems like a flaky idea from headquarters that might be abandoned any month. Remind them regularly that the campaign is here to stay and that top management is committed.

5. Introduce your partner. Your middlemen may be working with your partner's local chapters to implement the campaign. Smooth the way by giving them as much information as possible ahead of time. Brief them about the nonprofit. Warn them about possible culture clashes. Make sure they clearly understand your goals as well as your partner's. Pass on any tips you've learned from your dealings with your partner that might foster a good working relationship. The more smoothly those two groups get along, the better the campaign will run.

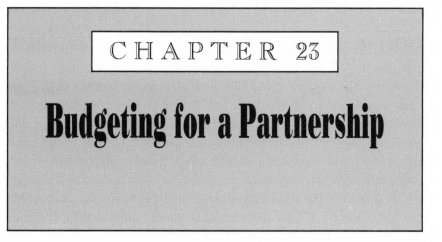

CHAPTER 23

Budgeting for a Partnership

What does a partnership cost? Obviously the costs vary enormously, depending on scale, duration, number of elements, and a host of other factors. Strictly marketing partnerships tend to cost about the same amount as traditional sales promotions, with a donation to the non-profit sometimes added to the mix. Your other costs—developing the campaign, creating materials, buying media, doing market research, and so on—remain essentially the same.

The donation to the nonprofit, in fact, represents the smallest part of the total expense. In 1989 Smirnoff Vodka donated $100,000 to Literacy Volunteers of America as part of a sponsored advertising campaign. The company then spent ten times that amount—$1 million—to promote the campaign. Smirnoff spent that much on promotion to maximize the campaign's visibility. Most companies spend two to three times the donation amount on advertising and promotion. And they consider that money well spent. After all, that's how they tell the world what they're doing. United Technologies, for example, allots a generous promotion budget to each of its arts sponsorships because, according to C. R. Hogan, Jr., manager of corporate contributions, "We look at it as the best way of protecting our investments in these organizations."

Which Pot to Pick?

One of the advantages of partnership campaigns is that companies have a wide range of choices when it comes to finding the funding. Money can come from the corporate giving budget as well as any number of business budgets. Most companies pull dollars from a variety of budgets, depending on which departments plan to benefit and which have the most to spend.

Money from the corporate giving budget is tax-deductible, which can be an incentive for companies that don't want to spend business dollars and want the deduction. However, money from business budgets is essentially tax-deductible as well, since it, too, comes out of earnings. Therefore, deductibility itself need not influence your funding decision.

Cautions

Two other concerns should influence your thinking. The first is that the source of funds can place additional pressure on the project to succeed if other programs suffer as a result. Therefore, it's wise to consider the potential backlash a program can unleash as you decide who's going to foot the bill.

The second is that corporate philanthropy money often has strings attached which may influence how that money is spent. Most corporate foundations are prohibited from self-dealing; their money must be spent on educational programs rather than programs that directly benefit the business. Companies deal with this restriction by using philanthropic money to donate to the nonprofit but using marketing funds to create the promotional elements of the campaign.

Budgeting Rules of Thumb

One of the hardest things about budgeting for a partnership campaign is the lack of certainty. Since you've never done it before, it's hard to know what you're getting into. Unexpected costs will no doubt crop up. It's best to think of partnerships the way you would any new program: you give it your best guess and then prepare for the worst.

To help newcomers to the process, we offer the following two crucial bits of advice:

1. Give yourself room. Take the program seriously and allocate a large enough budget to make it a significant part of your overall marketing program. Give it the advertising and promotional support it needs to succeed. Don't inhibit its chance to fly by clipping its wings at the start.

2. Give yourself flexibility. The only sure thing about a partnership campaign is that it will cost more than you thought. So plan for contingencies. Give yourself room to make mistakes, to change your mind, to realize partway through that there's a better way to do things. These flip-flops may be costly in the short term. But it's hoped that they'll pay off in the ultimate success of the program. Certainly they'll pay off in future campaigns, since you'll enter those with valuable experience under your belt.

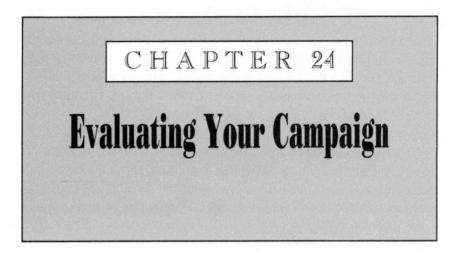

CHAPTER 24

Evaluating Your Campaign

In September 1991, the Tall Hills Multiple Sclerosis Society (not its real name) decided to mount a fund-raising dinner. The society hired a caterer, rented a ballroom, and sent out invitations. It spent $15,000 orchestrating the event. On the appointed night, hundreds of people arrived, wearing furs and smiling warmly. Speeches were made. Pictures were taken. Checks were signed. When the staff retired to their office and counted the money they found they had raised $12,000. "But," said the director, only slightly apologetic, "we got such good PR!"

Pretty questionable evaluation, wouldn't you say? But before you write this off as silly, unbusinesslike, nonprofit behavior, you should know that a lot of companies do exactly the same thing in evaluating their partnership campaigns. Instead of holding themselves accountable to the marketing goals they established early on, they write off the programs as strictly PR. Why? Not because the programs fail. Just because the companies fail to take them seriously. Usually they failed to set comprehensive goals for the programs back at the beginning, so they don't have evaluation criteria when they get to the end.

These companies are missing the boat. Since they don't evaluate their programs, they have no way of knowing how well they performed: where they surpassed expectations, where they fell short, or how to improve next time. They don't know how the public perceived the campaigns, or how their employees responded. They can only guess at the programs' impact on sales, at whether they boosted traffic or excited the sales force. And what about the nonprofits? They raised some money—but did they gain any new donors? Any volunteers? Any converts to the cause?

Without evaluation, there's no way to know the answers. Pretty foolhardy, given the amount of money these companies spent. And since they evaluate their other marketing campaigns, why not evaluate this one? As we said, some businesses make some pretty unbusinesslike mistakes. Let's hope your company isn't one of them.

Evaluation by the Goals

If you've been doing partnership by the book (this book!), you've done the hardest work of evaluation already. You did it back at the beginning when you set your goals. You decided at that time what you wanted your program to achieve. Now it's just a matter of learning whether it did.

You'll be evaluating it according to numerous criteria—as many criteria as you included in your goals. Did you have specific sales objectives? You'll have to measure sales results. Did you outline objectives for employee involvement? You'll have to communicate with employees to get their feedback. Did you hope to build awareness of your company in a new geographic market? You'll have to do market research in that area to find out who noticed. You want to evaluate your campaign the same way you would any conventional sales promotion program—and then tack on a number of other measures, because partnership isn't just a sales promotion.

Depending on your campaign's goals, here are some things you may be looking for:

1. Sales results: What was the impact of the campaign on sales volume? on market share? on average purchase quantity and frequency? on brand switching? on trial and repeat purchase behavior? on retail distribution intensity? on coupon redemption or proof-of-purchase returns? on store and warehouse shipments?

2. Target market results: Did heightened sales activity occur in the markets—geographic, socioeconomic, etc.—that you targeted?

3. Retail activity: What feedback did you get from retailers, distributors, and franchisees? What did they hear from their customers? What did they read in their local press? What feedback did you get from your sales force? What was the level of retail merchandising activity? What suggestions do these people have for improving future campaigns?

4. Publicists: How much coverage did you get? Was it where you wanted it? Was it favorable? What will you do differently next time?

5. Employee attitudes: Did employees get involved in the campaign? What were their comments? Will they continue to support your partner? What are their thoughts about how the campaign could be improved? What surprised you about employee involvement?

6. Management attitudes: Did your managers support the campaign? What are their suggestions for future campaigns?

7. Public reaction: How did the public respond to the campaign? Did it respond favorably to your choice of cause and partner? Did your actions seem credible or were they perceived as a marketing gimmick? Did the campaign have an impact on your corporate image? on the image of your products or services? Would the public support an extended campaign on this issue? with this partner? Use market research to find out.

8. Revenue/expense results: What does a cost-benefit analysis tell you about the campaign?

9. Working relationship: How was your working relationship with your partner? What would have made it smoother?

10. Internal campaign management: What worked well in the way the campaign was managed? What would have made it smoother?

Ask people at every level for answers to these questions—especially salespeople, retailers, and front-line employees. They were in the best position to see the campaign in action; make sure to learn what they learned.

Earlier in this book (page 164) we suggested you place your partnership goals on a grid to determine which were the most important. Keep that grid in mind as you do your evaluation. Presumably you designed the campaign accordingly. Don't change your expectations now that it's over.

Evaluate the Campaign with Your Partner

Some companies are squeamish about sharing their results with their partners. Don't be. This was a joint campaign. You entered it for common gain. Neither could have done it without the other. Now evaluate it together. Learn together what worked and what didn't. If you intend to work together again, this learning is crucial. If you don't, it will help you both work better with other partners in the future.

Here are some things to consider in evaluating your partner's side of the program:

   1. **Money:** How much money did your partner get? Was it what you had hoped for? What would have increased the take?

   2. **Exposure:** How much press coverage did your partner get? Was it in the "right" places? Was the "right" message given out?

   3. **Public response:** What did the organization hear from its members? from its donors? Did donations increase? Did the organization sign up new members? Did it recruit new volunteers? Did it receive more requests for information? Did the campaign have an impact on its image? on its credibility? How does the general public feel about the organization's participation in the campaign? Pay for market research to find out.

   4. **The cause:** What benefits accrued to the cause as a result

of the campaign? Did it improve the public's knowledge or awareness of the issue? Again, pay for market research to find out.

5. Cost-benefit analysis: Was the campaign worth doing,
given the opportunity cost?

6. Working relationship: How does the organization feel
about the partnership? What would have made it smoother?

7. Internal management: How does the organization think
the campaign was handled internally? What does it hear from its
local chapters? What would have made it smoother?

As with any promotion, it's hard to isolate the effects of one program. Did sales gains and increased volunteer interest really come
from this campaign? It's hard to know. The market is shaped by
countless forces, so assigning a definitive cause and effect is tricky.
That's one more reason to think about waging an extended campaign
with a long-term partner. That gives the public repeated opportunities
to respond and lets you measure results over a longer period. This is
especially important in measuring image gains, which accrue gradually.

Also, your first campaign may not turn out to be everything you
hoped. Some campaigns are more successful than others, even for the
pros. American Express raised $4 million for local charities with its
1985 Project Hometown America campaign—but card use and new
card purchases increased only marginally. Overall, though, the company's numerous cause-related marketing campaigns have contributed
greatly to both the business results and the image of the company. So
amortize your risks and increase your opportunities for gain by making
public purpose partnering an integral part of your operation.

CHAPTER 25

Putting It All Together: A Hypothetical Campaign

I was sixty-six years old. I still had to make a living. I looked at my Social Security check of $105 and decided to use that to try to franchise my chicken recipe. Folks had always liked my chicken.

—Colonel Harland Sanders

What does a piggybacked campaign look like in practice? Let's put one together so that you can see the thinking from start to finish. In fact, let's put together two campaigns—one that works and one that doesn't. There's a lot to be learned from bad examples, especially in public purpose partnering, where many companies make the same mistakes. So we'll look at a hypothetical campaign that backfired, and then reconstruct it to make it work.

For the purpose of this example, let's create a small chain of up-scale grocery stores called Bob's Basket. You've been in stores like Bob's. The produce counter displays seven types of lettuce. The shelves stock Dijon mustard but not French's. The butchers wear red-and-white-checked aprons and name tags. The store's monthly newsletter features environmentally friendly products and recipes us-

ing sun-dried tomatoes. Bob's hallmarks are quality, service, and premium prices.

Let's also give Bob's some background and some marketing goals.
The chain opened in Los Angeles in 1985 and quickly spread to San
Francisco, San Jose, and Sacramento. By 1989 it had opened stores
in Portland, Seattle, and Chicago; by 1991 it was preparing its East
Coast launch. In each city, the stores were located in thriving retail
areas near, but not in, downtown; their target market was the young-
to-middle-aged professionals who lived and worked in those neighborhoods. Despite a lot of competition in the upscale grocery market,
Bob's Basket was a strong player in every city, with a healthy share
of the market.

Now, as the company planned its East Coast launch, managers
contemplated adding a public purpose element to their marketing efforts. Supporting a social cause would fit with the personal beliefs of
the store's owners and employees, it would appeal to the clientele,
and it could become an integral part of Bob's image as the chain became a national entity. Over the years, the company had dabbled in
philanthropy, giving small amounts to a variety of causes, but had
never thought strategically about those donations. Its partnership
campaign would require starting from square one. What social issue
should it pick? What nonprofit organization? What should be the elements of the campaign? Store managers weighed the possibilities.

Everyone decided quickly that whatever cause they picked, the
campaign should be long-term. Durability would indicate the company's
sincerity: "It shouldn't just look like a marketing gimmick," they
agreed. Durability would also strongly identify the company with the
issue. "We want customers to think, 'Bob's: the store that cares
about X,' when they think of us," said one of the marketing managers, and that became the goal of the campaign.

They also quickly decided to target "the hungry" as a campaign
theme: they believed that customers who were buying food for themselves would respond to the chance to help others in need. The choice
of a nonprofit was a little tougher: should they go local, partnering a
food bank in each city? No: now that the company was national, they
believed they needed a national partner. But none of the national agencies they could think of had the instant name recognition and image of

quality they wanted associated with the stores. Ultimately they settled on CARE, an international food distribution agency with a long history and a well-established reputation. Bob's managers felt comfortable with those traits, and believed their customers would respond.

Their next decision was how to structure the campaign. They liked the idea of a cause-related marketing scheme—helping the cause and their sales at the same time. So they decided that for every $25 purchase, they would give $1 to CARE. The campaign would go on indefinitely as a sign of the company's serious commitment, and would be advertised in print ads and point-of-purchase displays. They decided to print a message about CARE on their grocery bags and to put leaflets about the organization at every cash register. These strategies, they thought, would make their commitment apparent and credible, and an integral part of the business. To kick off the campaign they held a press conference at which they presented CARE with a check for $5,000. The story appeared on the business page of the local paper in most of their cities.

Campaign Results from Hunger

Unfortunately, the campaign didn't pan out the way Bob's managers had anticipated. Consumers just didn't respond in a big way. Oh, they were sympathetic. Clerks got positive comments about the program and shoppers were happy their purchases were helping CARE. But the program had no noticeable effect on sales. Despite the large advertising campaign, traffic figures held steady. Despite the point-of-purchase displays, sales figures showed no appreciable gain. After several months, Bob's ran discount coupons in local papers, hoping to increase response. The coupons offered a discount on selected products which would trigger an additional donation to CARE. Customers redeemed the coupons—but at the typical redemption rate. The CARE connection didn't have a measurable impact.

After a year of tinkering with the program, managers decided to call it quits. The program wasn't working and they didn't know why. Maybe the grocery business wasn't designed for public purpose marketing. Maybe customers were tired of the cause-related approach. Certainly the marketing managers were tired of it, and had better things to do besides. The first East Coast store had opened and was demanding their attention. So almost a year to the day from the date of the press conference, Bob's quietly ended its public purpose marketing campaign. Managers say maybe one day they'll try again: they like the idea of helping a social cause while boosting sales. The employees seemed to like it. But for some reason, this time it just didn't seem to work.

Why Did Bob's Campaign Fall Flat?

What was the problem with Bob's campaign? Is it true that the grocery business can't support public purpose partnerships? Or that customers are tired of helping a worthy cause? Hardly. The problem with Bob's campaign was that it was poorly conceived. Bob's managers took a great idea and ruined it with a couple of poor decisions. Let's dissect the campaign and find out why. Then let's reconstruct it to make it work.

Goals

Bob's managers made a critical mistake right up front. They failed to delineate their goals. Whom did they want to reach—what income group? what geographic group? What did they want to achieve: new business? repeat business? Partnership campaigns should support specific goals—not just generate warm fuzzy feelings. Had Bob's managers planned theirs strategically, they could have designed a campaign that worked. As it was, they were doomed to fail because they didn't know where they were going. Had the managers looked through their marketing, philanthropic, and human resource goals, they might have come up with a list like this:

1. Business goals: the campaign should:
   - increase customer loyalty to our stores. We want to become our customers' *regular* supermarket.
   - woo customers from the competition. We want to attract upscale, urban professionals and residents.
   - increase walk-in traffic in each store. We want to encourage new people to try our stores.
   - encourage people to spend more money in the stores.
2. Image goals: the campaign should:
   - strengthen each store's image as "the neighborhood store."
   - reinforce the company's image of quality and service.
   - show that Bob's cares about its community, not just about profits.
3. Social goals: the campaign should have a demonstrable effect on a social problem of concern to our customers.
4. Employee goals: the campaign should:
   - enable employees to participate in a social cause through volunteering.
   - give employees the feeling that they can help make a difference on a social problem.
   - build employees' loyalty to the company.
5. Exposure: the campaign should be unusual and mediagenic in order to attract media attention in each local market. It should attract at least one feature story in every local paper, and, if possible, a mention on the local evening news.

Choice of Issue

Hunger and food store: a good match or a forced connection? Good match! Bob's managers played it right on this one. There is a tight and logical fit between the issue and the business. They were right to think their customers would respond to a chance to feed the needy while stocking up themselves. But they were lucky. They should have checked this out with market research. Relying on instinct can be dangerous in picking an issue because you're apt to choose your own preference, rather than your customers'.

Choice of Partner

Who cares about CARE? Lots of people do—and thank goodness they send checks. But the majority of people on the streets of Los Angeles? of Chicago? of a big East Coast city? They care more about the people they step over every day as they walk into Bob's stores— the hungry and homeless in their own backyards. Those people are a major problem to them: one they wish they didn't encounter daily, one they wish they could do something about. Bob's had a chance to address that concern—but passed on the opportunity. Instead Bob's picked a partner that was worthy—but invisible. CARE is a great choice as a philanthropy recipient—but for a marketing partner, it's weak.

Bob's broke one of the most fundamental rules of public purpose marketing: match the geography of your partner to the geography of your markets. The company needed a local campaign, not a national one. The managers wanted to strengthen each store's ties to its neighborhood, not remind their customers they were shopping at a national chain. A local partner would have tugged much more directly at customers' heartstrings. It would also have offered con- crete opportunities for getting employees, customers, and the press involved.

The logical partner would have been a food bank or homeless shel- ter in each city with a Bob's store. Again, market research—even just informal polling of customers and prospective customers—would have helped Bob's make an effective choice. Unfortunately, Bob's market- ers—who routinely use research in designing their sales campaigns— put their good sense aside and became *philanthropists* with their marketing program.

Developing the Campaign

Suppose Bob's had done market research and had picked a local homeless shelter in every city with a store. Now what? What should the campaign include? Bob's selected some good elements: a cause- related marketing campaign, information on the bags, a generous do- nation. What went wrong? Not much—but more things could have gone right. Had Bob's probed its business areas more thoroughly, it could have come up with numerous other campaign elements which might have generated more interest and enthusiasm from customers and the media. Bob's also could have tied the campaign to its goals in a much more powerful way. For instance, had Bob's managers looked at the total menu of partnership options and brainstormed possibilities in each, they might have come up with a list like this:

Strategic philanthropy: What could Bob's do here? The stores could give each shelter a $1,000 donation. For $2,000 more than the $5,000 gift to CARE, they could have made a significant contribution in each of their seven cities.

Cause-related marketing: What could Bob's do here? Several things.

1. *$.25 per bag:* In the CARE campaign, Bob's gave $1 to CARE for every $25 purchase. A nice gesture. Doesn't do much for people who spend less than $25, though. And doesn't do much for walk-in traffic, which Bob's was trying to encourage. A better strategy would be to donate $.25 to the shelter for every *bag* of groceries purchased. Decreasing the size of the purchase would make it easier for shoppers to contribute. It would enable walk-ins to participate, since they are unlikely to spend $25. And it would have little impact on Bob's overall donation.

2. *"Bob's Coupons":* Had the managers probed a little further, they might have come up with a second cause-related marketing strategy. For every bag of groceries purchased, customers could choose to get a Bob's Coupon, good for a free meal at the local homeless shelter, which they could give out to panhandlers. The coupon would support the campaign's goals in two ways. One, it would encourage homeless people to use the shelters, giving them more help than a handout. Two, it would give customers who feel uncomfortable when approached by a street person an easy, positive response.

Special events: What could Bob's do here? Again, several things.

1. *A contest:* The chain could hold a monthlong contest among Bob's stores to see which store could generate the biggest donation

to its local shelter. This would build customer loyalty to the neighborhood store, encourage repeat business, and serve Bob's marketing goal of encouraging customers to see Bob's as their regular grocery store.

2. *Holiday events:* Bob's could hold special holiday events designed to trigger additional donations. For instance: at Thanksgiving they could offer to make an additional donation to the shelter for every turkey bought. They could donate a turkey to the shelter for every 100 turkeys bought. They could give each turkey-buying customer a number so that the customer would feel he or she was contributing.

3. *Family events:* To build business with families, Bob's could hold "family days" at the stores, with specials on children's food items, cooking demonstrations geared to kids, easy-to-make recipes on cards, etc. Children who brought donations of nonperishable food items would trigger an additional donation to the shelter.

Premiums: What could Bob's do here? It's hard to think of a premium product that a homeless shelter could produce. Let's move on to the next partnership option.

Licensing: What could Bob's do here? Again, not much. Licensing doesn't lend itself to a partnership with a homeless shelter, either. Let's keep going.

Sponsored ads: Bingo. There's lots that Bob's could do here.

1. *Add a message to their ads:* They could include a message about homelessness in each of their ads, designed to educate the public about the issue.

2. *Advertise success:* They could take out ads to advertise milestones in their campaign. For instance: the day that Bob's and its customers fed the one thousandth person at the shelter; the day that Bob's and its customers donated $100,000 through their cause-related marketing campaign; the day that Bob's and its customers donated $1 million worth of food. These milestones would let the public and the customers know the campaign was working.

3. *In-store advertising:* Bob's could place educational messages about homelessness on its grocery bags and on in-store displays. The

store could put articles about people who work and stay at the shelter in the company newsletter and on the bulletin board.

4. *Slogan:* Bob's could develop a campaign slogan, such as "Help Bob's Help the Homeless." The slogan could appear on everything: aprons, grocery bags, signs, trucks. Everywhere it appeared there would be a short message educating the public about the issue—and reminding customers about Bob's commitment to the cause.

Vendor relationships: What could Bob's do here? How about hire people from the shelter for day jobs—gathering shopping carts, guiding cars in the parking lot? There are labor issues to consider: because of union regulations or seniority issues this may not be possible. But it's worth investigating. Hiring people from the shelter could enable Bob's to help its adopted cause in a very direct way.

Employee volunteers: What could Bob's do here? Again, lots.

1. *Encourage volunteering:* At the very least, Bob's could encourage its employees to volunteer at the shelter. To support a volunteer campaign, it could print stories about volunteers in the company newsletter and post them on each store's bulletin board.

2. *"Bob's Night":* The stores could also hold an annual or semi-annual "Bob's Night" at the shelter, when all store employees (wearing Bob's aprons) would cook and serve dinner using food donated by Bob's.

In-kind donations: What could Bob's do here?

1. *Food donations:* Each Bob's store could donate all its less-than-fresh food to the local shelter. Not only is this tax-deductible, it reinforces Bob's message that it sells only the best.

2. *Customer donations:* Bob's could encourage its customers to support the shelter by placing a barrel for customer's donations of canned and packaged goods in each store.

3. *"Bob's Coupons":* Bob's could sell Bob's Coupons at each cash register for $.25 so that customers could buy as many as they wish and hand them out to homeless people on the street. Bob's would support the free meals by donating food to the shelter.

Media exposure: How could Bob's generate media interest? It shouldn't be too difficult. The unusual nature of some of these events would attract the press. Bob's would just need to be systematic in calling attention to them. Imagine, for instance, the visual impact of all Bob's employees, wearing Bob's aprons, cooking and serving at the local shelter. Or the donation of hundreds of turkeys the day before Thanksgiving—a donation made possible by Bob's customers. Or the story of the one thousandth person fed thanks to Bob's customers' patronage. These are the kinds of positive stories the media like to cover. They are tailor-made for closing bits on the local evening news, and for feature pieces in the "life-style" section of the local paper.

Rolling out the campaign: Each of these elements could be rolled out sequentially to create a long-term campaign. The program might kick off with the cash donations, followed by the continuing cause-related marketing campaign. Sponsored ads would announce the campaign to the public. Several months later, Bob's might introduce another element, say "Family Days" or holiday events. Again, several months later the stores could hold "Bob's Night" at the shelter. After a pause of several more months, a series of sponsored ads might announce campaign milestones or tell stories about employee volunteers. By staggering the events and publicizing each one, Bob's could easily keep this campaign going for years. Of course, the stores should monitor customer response through sales and traffic data and through questionnaires. And they should adjust the campaign in response to what they learn.

All of these elements are strategically designed to meet Bob's specific marketing, philanthropy, and human resource goals. But they also have other benefits. They give each store—managers and employees—a sense of autonomy in its campaign. They help Bob's customers deal concretely with a problem they encounter every day. By working the social issue into many facets of Bob's business, they enable the company to have a real impact on the problem. Unlike the poorly conceived campaign Bob's managers came up with, this campaign should work.

Rules of Thumb for Developing a Public Purpose Partnership

1. For a partnership to succeed, your company must be committed to the strategy from senior management down.

2. Use market research to select the cause and your partners and to develop the program elements.

3. Make sure there is a logical association among the cause, your partner, and your product or service.

4. Make sure there is a match among your target markets, your partner's constituency, and the geographic reach of the program.

5. Develop a good working relationship with your partner by emphasizing open communication and contractual agreements.

6. Commit sufficient resources, attention, and priority to the program.

7. Be committed to the cause: its gain is your gain. The public will sense insincerity.

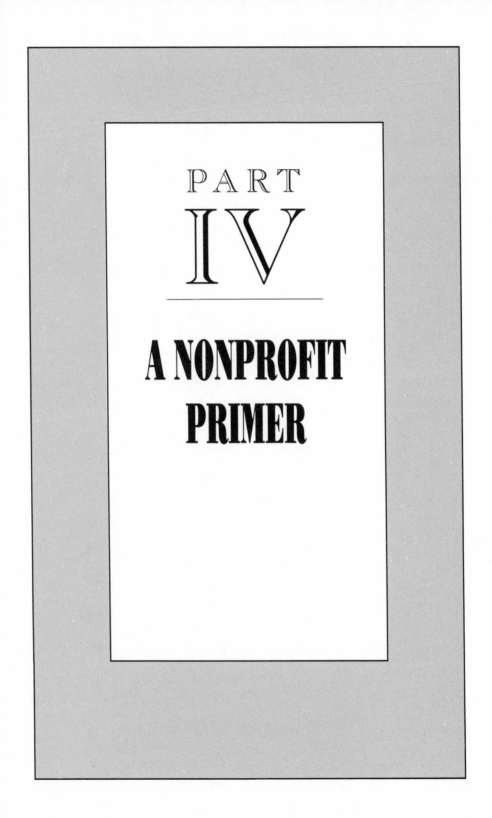

PART
IV

A NONPROFIT PRIMER

Nonprofits 101

Working with a nonprofit is a little like going to a foreign country where the people speak English. At first everything looks pretty familiar. There are obvious differences, of course: cars drive on the "wrong" side of the road; they eat porridge instead of corn flakes; they wear "braces" where we wear suspenders. But you smile at those eccentricities: they're charming deviations in people who are otherwise kindred spirits. It's only as you stick around—read the papers, watch the "telly," get to know a "bloke" or two—that you realize that the differences go deeper than you'd originally thought.

What's different, of course, is the culture—the values, the outlooks, the ways of approaching problems, the ways of relating to people—the millions of invisible things that make the country what it is. And of course precisely because they're invisible, those are the things that trip you up. You laugh at the wrong lines, you speak at the wrong moments, you move ahead when others wait and wait when others move ahead. Before long, you find yourself thinking, "It's so frustrating in this country! Why don't they do things the way we do?"

Eventually, if you're flexible, you realize that the key to a successful visit is to learn a little of the culture and to stop expecting everything to be like home. Once you do that, you can appreciate the differences and get the most out of your visit.

Working with a nonprofit is similar. The outward differences—

smaller offices, smaller budgets, smaller salaries—mask more fundamental cultural differences underneath. Those differences are not im-
penetrable. In fact, they are quite negotiable. Some of them—like the
nonprofit focus on mission—are the reason you've chosen to partner
a nonprofit in the first place. With a little patience and a little guid-
ance, you should navigate quite smoothly. To help you, we offer a
"travel guide" to the world of nonprofits.

Mission First, Money Second

The first thing that separates nonprofits from for-profits is a very
different sense of mission. For corporations, "mission" means profit.
Profits are the goal of the business. Ultimately they drive all decisions.

For nonprofits, "mission" has a very different meaning. It has
nothing to do with money and everything to do with saving the world.
Whether it's educating children, supporting people with AIDS, saving
baby seals, or performing a symphony, what drives nonprofit staffs,
boards, and volunteers is the belief that by doing what they do, they
make the world a better place.

That's not to say that nonprofit people are self-important. (If anything, their often precarious finances keep them humble.) Rather it's
to say that most nonprofit people believe very strongly in what they
do. That's why they do it—certainly not for the money, which is considerably less than they would make in the for-profit world. This belief
in what they do colors all their thinking. It is the yardstick against
which all decisions are measured. It becomes, in effect, their bottom
line.

Money Matters

To say that nonprofits are mission-driven is not to say that they
don't think about money. On the contrary, they think about money all
the time. Mostly they think about where to get it. The chronic need

to raise money—and the concomitant constraints on operations—are major shapers of nonprofit culture.

Even for large, entrepreneurial nonprofits, funding is a major concern. Money comes from a variety of sources, most of them uncontrollable. Grants are subject to the whim of the funding agency—government, foundation, or corporation. Individual donations must be solicited anew each year. Memberships and program fees are relatively stable, but cover only a portion of expenses. As a result, a great deal of time and energy is spent considering where the next dollars will come from. This is done primarily by the executive director, with help in medium to large nonprofits from the development director or development department. But even people at the low end of the organization feel the ebb and flow of budget worries as programs are added and cut with each year's changing income.

This chronic shortage of money has understandable repercussions on nonprofit staffing. The most obvious is nonprofits' reliance on volunteers. This is generally not a matter of choice; paid staff are far easier to manage. But money being what it is, and necessity being the mother of invention, most nonprofits have become skillful volunteer managers. They have learned how to recruit desirable volunteers and train them, how to motivate them, how to evaluate them regularly and positively, and how to compensate them effectively with education, respect, meaningful work, and appreciation. They have also accepted the fact that working with volunteers means things happen more slowly, require more patient explanation, and need more group buy-in than they would if the staff were all paid.

The second repercussion of chronically tight budgets is understaffing. Amost all nonprofits are seriously understaffed, with most people working very long hours, often doing more than one job. Their loyalty to the institution and to the cause tends to keep them in their jobs, but staff burnout is a chronic problem. Nonprofits also tend to have many part-time staff, in part to reduce costs by keeping salaries lower, and in part to accommodate women who want to spend time at home with their children.

Decision by Committee

Decisions in nonprofits often require consensus. Committees—of the board, of staff, of volunteers—are often involved, and actions may be belabored or postponed if an important person is unavailable. Be warned: at some point in your partnership you'll want a decision fast and your partner will be unable to comply. This often becomes a sore point in corporate-nonprofit partnerships. Flexibility is needed on both sides.

How Nonprofits View Corporate Partnerships

Most nonprofits will approach a corporate partnership with mixed feelings. On the one hand, they want the benefits the partnership can offer. On the other, they are fearful of appearing too commercial, of appearing to have sold out to a corporation in exchange for cash. Don't misunderstand: this fear is not based on dislike for money or for business. It is based on a nonprofit's overwhelming concern for its integrity.

Nonprofit Integrity

Integrity is a nonprofit's most valuable possession. It is the thing the organization cherishes—and protects—above all else. This is vital to understand if you are going to work with a nonprofit, because there is nothing quite like it in the for-profit world, yet it will be at the heart of your negotiations.

A nonprofit's concern with its integrity is similar to, but different from, a company's concern about its image. You carefully cultivate your image, you try to protect it from bad press, you hope it represents you well to the world. But corporate images are created with advertising. If need be, they can be altered with a new campaign.

They are in some ways external to the company itself. A nonprofit's integrity, on the other hand, is its soul and essence. It is the reason people believe in the organization; it is the reason people give it money. If a nonprofit's integrity is sullied, at worst, the organization's existence may be threatened. At best, heads—of the director, the board, the staff—will roll.

What exactly is nonprofit integrity? It is a combination of things. It is the nonprofit's image, the way it appears to the public. It is the organization's reputation for doing what it does well and honestly. It is what the organization represents: the hope that whatever problem it is tackling will be solved. But most important, it is the fact that the organization does what it does for *public gain,* not for the benefit of private individuals. Because of that, the public believes in the organization and trusts it. And that trust must not be betrayed. It is to preserve that trust that nonprofits guard their integrity so jealously.

Of course, that is precisely where nonprofits differ from corporations. Corporations *do* exist for private gain, and are not trusted by the public the same way. That's one of the reasons partnerships benefit you—and it's precisely what nonprofits fear. They fear that by working closely with you, they will appear to be doing what they are doing for money, rather than for the public good—that your offer of money will appear to have swayed them from their "pure, altruistic" mission and, as a result, made their programs less trustworthy.

Obviously this fear doesn't stop many nonprofits from engaging in partnerships. But it does create requirements which their partners must meet. Most nonprofits require that their partners' products and services be compatible with their mission (no cigarette companies for the Cancer Society) and that the campaign be designed to promote their mission by getting the word out to promote their cause. If you understand their needs in this regard, you'll find dealing with a nonprofit partner much easier.

Implied Endorsements

The way nonprofits guard their integrity is by being fiercely protective of their names and logos. How those items are used—where they appear, for how long, etc.—is of great concern, and rightly so.

They have everything to lose if a logo is used inappropriately. Of greatest concern is that a nonprofit's name and logo will be used to imply endorsement of a company's product or service. Virtually no nonprofit will agree to that. Nonprofits see it as the surest way to threaten the trust placed in them by their members, funders, and supporters.

Nonprofits generally try to avoid implied endorsements by avoiding partnerships with companies that make products they clearly don't want to endorse, or by asking that partnership materials include the company name rather than a product name. Of course, your company may want the implied endorsement; that may be one of the reasons you sought the relationship. But as you negotiate your partnership terms, you'll need to be sensitive to your partner's concerns. It may help to remember that you've sought this partner because you want to associate with its integrity and image. It is, therefore, in your interest as well to keep that image uncommercial.

Implied Endorsements: Procter & Gamble and the Arthritis Foundation

Unfortunately, implied endorsements are just that—implications—and sometimes even the best intentions can't prevent them. Procter & Gamble found this out when it developed a partnership with the Arthritis Foundation.

In 1989 P&G had just developed a new plastic snap top for its king-size box of Tide. As an employee of the company played with the lid one day, he realized that it was exceptionally easy to open and close; that, in fact, this might be the only detergent box someone with arthritis in his or her hands could open and close without help. So the company approached the Arthritis Foundation to see whether it would be interested in a partnership. The foundation agreed. Partnership with the giant consumer goods manufacturer would meet several of its needs. The organization was interested in achieving greater visibility with the public; with a public recognition factor of just 2 percent, it welcomed exposure for its name and logo. The foundation also welcomed the cash. So the two organizations agreed on a yearlong arrangement in which the new Tide box would bear the nonprofit's logo and the words "commended by the Arthritis Foundation." In addition, P&G did two Sunday-newspaper coupon promotions in which it offered a percentage of all Tide sales to the foundation. The foundation netted $200,000.

All seemed well until the company started getting phone calls from people who wanted to know how Tide could help their arthritis. The company had to explain that it was not the product that was commended, but merely the packaging. Despite the organizations' best efforts to make the "commendation" clear, it was still misunderstood by a number of customers. As someone at the foundation later said, "You know, perception is reality. As long as our logo was there, no matter what we said, some people were going to perceive what they wanted to believe."

What Nonprofits Want from a Partnership

Nonprofits want three things from a corporate partnership. You can think of them as the three M's: money, message, and members.

- **Money:** Money is by far the most valuable return from a partnership campaign. It is made even more valuable by the fact that in most campaigns, unless the corporation deems otherwise, the money is unrestricted. That is, the nonprofit can use it however it wants. This is different from most nonprofit income streams, which are earmarked for special projects. Whereas grants are usually given for a new ballet, a particular environmental campaign, a particular program for inner-city teens, or some other specially designated project, unrestricted cash can be used to pay the rent, the utility bill, even the staff.
- **Message:** The mission is the message. That's why nonprofits exist. Whether it's teaching about tropical rain forests or working to end a disease, the nonprofit's mission means getting a message out to the public. And that's exactly what partnership campaigns are designed to do. With all the marketing resources of a corporation behind it, a nonprofit can reach many more people than it would ever reach on its own.
- **Members:** To keep themselves going, nonprofits depend on

individual members. These people are the lifeblood of the organization: they pay dues, they volunteer, they write their congresspeople,
they support the organization's work so that it can advance its goals.
By reaching thousands or even millions of people with the nonprofit's
message, a partnership campaign can win new members for the
organization.

What They Will Ask

Nonprofits will have several concerns going into a corporate partnership. These are the kinds of questions they will ask themselves—and
you—as they consider doing a campaign.

- **Mission-related:** Does this venture help us in our mission? (If the answer is no, most nonprofits will choose not to participate for fear the venture will jeopardize their IRS tax-exempt
status, offend supporters, and divert them from their regular responsibilities.)
- **Corporate reputation:** Is this corporation one we want
to be associated with? Do we approve of their products or services? Are they the subject of any public controversy? Are they
socially responsible? Are they a suitable image match for us?
- **Implied endorsements:** Can we partner this company
without appearing to endorse its products? How can the campaign
be designed accordingly?
- **Existing relationships:** Will entering this partnership
jeopardize our relationships with other funders—other corporations, foundations, major donors, our members?
- **Negative press potential:** Can this partnership reflect
badly on us in any way?
- **Commercialization vs. credibility:** Will we lose our
credibility by doing this? Will we appear to be selling out by selling
our name?
- **Responsibilities:** What will our responsibilities be? How
much time will this take from our regular duties?
- **Money:** How much money are we likely to make? What's

the minimum? Maximum? Are there any guarantees? Will we have any costs?

- **Control:** Will we have control over how our name and logo are used? Will we be able to review all campaign material?
- **Audience:** Who will this campaign reach? Are those our target audiences?

How One Nonprofit Does It: The American Cancer Society

For years, the American Cancer Society (ACS) eschewed corporate partnerships because of concern about implied endorsements. But recently the organization changed its mind. ACS believes that partnerships hold too many opportunities for raising money and for promoting its message to pass them up. So with a new corporate relations staff person heading the effort, the society is now exploring avenues for corporate partnership and formulating policies that will help it protect its integrity. It is looking carefully at how it can select partners, structure the partnerships, and avoid the problem of implied endorsements.

Picking Partners

ACS is regularly approached by companies that want to create partnerships. The society turns down 95 percent of these requests because the company or the proposed partnership is unsuitable. To be considered for partnership, a company must meet two requirements:

- The company and its products must be compatible with the society's mission. ACS will not partner a company that produces unhealthy food, tobacco or alcohol products, or any product that counters its mission of promoting a healthy life-style.
- The company must be well established. ACS wants to know

its partners can deliver the goods. The society also believes that its partners' images reflect on them. So it chooses companies whose stature and image are on a par with its own.

Structuring the Relationship

Many of the requests ACS receives are rejected because they are exploitative. They come from companies that want to use the ACS name to sell their product, but offer little in return. Or they want to sell to the ACS donor list, a practice the society prohibits. Or they propose returns that are too small for the effort required; for example, a yearlong nationwide promotion netting the society only $5,000 to $10,000. For ACS to agree to a partnership, the campaign must provide a significant amount of money, and it must genuinely promote the society's message and mission.

As of this writing, ACS is planning a two-year partnership which meets both of these requirements with Doncaster, a women's clothing manufacturer. Rather than selling retail, Doncaster distributes its clothing through a network of "fashion consultants," women who sell the clothing out of their homes. Four times a year, the company sends consultants new wardrobes. The consultants then schedule private showings with friends and associates. In the ACS partnership, Doncaster will buy educational material from the society about cancers common to women. The company will distribute the material to its fashion consultants, who will discuss it with their clients. In addition, Doncaster will donate to the society $1 from every sale. In this way, the society will net a significant financial return, a projected $400,000 to $500,000. It will also have its message promoted in a very direct way.

Avoiding Implied Endorsements

The Doncaster partnership is also exemplary in that it completely avoids the problem of implied endorsements. Since there are no links between clothing and cancer, there is no implication that ACS endorses Doncaster clothes as good for preventing the disease. But the society realizes that partnership opportunities will arise with companies whose products are not so clearly removed from cancer. Food companies, for instance, would make natural partners, especially as food manufacturers continue to make health claims for their products. Would ACS agree to partner a company that makes vitamin supplements? Probably not—because although the society doesn't disapprove of vitamin supplements, it prefers to stress the importance of eating a balanced diet. What about a cereal manufacturer? Possibly—if the cereal was healthful and if the society could adequately explain its position to the public.

In any campaign with the potential for an implied endorsement, explaining its position will be something the society insists on. It will require that the relationship between the society and the company be clearly spelled out in campaign material; for example, "X company will donate Y cents to ACS for every coupon redeemed." And in some campaigns the society may insist on a disclaimer, stating that ACS does not endorse the product. But ACS also realizes that ultimately it can't control what consumers thinks. Occasionally, despite careful choices and disclaimers, some consumers may take the ACS name on a commercial label as an endorsement of that product. The Society won't be happy, but is willing to take the risk in order to reap the benefits of public purpose partnerships.

A Nonprofit Glossary

Since nonprofit culture is different from corporate culture, it's not surprising that the language is a bit different, too. Here are some key words and phrases for corporate travelers venturing into the nonprofit world.

corporate term	nonprofit equivalent
profit	surplus revenue, excess revenue, revenue over expenses

When a business makes a profit, that money is reinvested in the business as retained earnings, or is distributed among the busi-

ness's owners or shareholders as dividends. Nonprofits do not have owners or shareholders. If they earn or raise more money than they spend in a given year, that money goes into the next year's operating budget. The word "profit" does not exist in nonprofit accounting practice. Rather, that money is called surplus revenue or one of the other terms above.

shareholders   ———

A business is owned by its shareholders. A nonprofit is not owned by anyone. It is managed in the public trust by a board of trustees. All money raised or earned is put back into the operating budget to run the organization's programs.

board of directors   board of trustees
                                                      (sometimes called
                                                      board of directors)

A corporation's directors are charged with overseeing the management of the company in the interest of its stockholders. A nonprofit's trustees are charged with overseeing the management of the nonprofit for the public. It is their job to make sure the organization is doing what it was chartered to do by the IRS.

president   executive director

vice-president for ———   assistant director for ———
                                                      or director of ———

CHAPTER 27

Entrepreneurial Nonprofits

Our nonprofit organizations are becoming America's management leaders. . . . They are practicing what American businesses only preach . . . working out the policies and practices that business will have to learn tomorrow.

—Peter F. Drucker, Marie Rankin Clarke Professor of Social Science and Management at The Claremont Graduate School Management Program

Nonprofits practicing what businesses only preach? Using today what business will learn tomorrow? This is hardly the standard thinking on nonprofits. Is Professor Drucker pulling our leg? Or is it time to sit up and take another look at the not-for-profit sector?

It is time indeed, because the last decade has brought huge changes. While corporations experienced their own spurts of growth and recession, nonprofits endured parallel turmoil. With nonprofit fortunes closely tied to the health of business and government, these organizations thrived in the early 1980s, but lost much of their traditional funding in the past few years. Some were forced to close. Others scaled back their programs. But many nonprofits used the opportunity to go back to the drawing board and rethink the ways they operate. These organizations emerged from the decade leaner and meaner, with new—businesslike—attitudes in place and new management practices on board. These newly *entrepreneurial* nonprofits are well positioned for success in the 1990s and beyond—and they will make powerful business partners for the corporations smart enough to seize the opportunity to work with them.

Let's take a look at the challenges that have faced nonprofits over the past few years—and the ways entrepreneurial nonprofits have responded.

Challenge #1: Government Cutbacks

Most nonprofits get the lion's share of their operating income from federal, state, and local governments. Governments mandate the provision of social services and pay nonprofits to deliver them. But the 1980s played havoc with this relatively dependable source of income. Over the decade, federal government grants decreased by 20 percent and nonprofit groups lost $30 billion in direct aid. Budget shortfalls at the state and local levels compounded the crisis.

So far, the 1990s are delivering more of the same. A total of $429 billion is being cut from the federal budget over the first half of the decade, much of that in spending for health and social programs. Similar cuts are being made at state and local levels. As a result, many nonprofit agencies have been forced to cut back on staff and services. Whole program areas have been eliminated, and the number of people being served has declined.

The entrepreneurial nonprofit response: Entrepreneurial nonprofits have seen the writing on the wall. Recognizing that government funds are unlikely to increase any time soon, they have developed revenue-producing lines of business to replace the lost income. These business ventures are designed to provide stable, continuing revenue. For example:

- A job training program which lost a large portion of its federal funding contracted with a private retail district in its city to provide street cleaning services in the downtown retail core. The long-term contract provides job training and employment opportunities for the organization's clients and provides stable, long-term income for the agency.

- A nonprofit hospital whose government subsidies no longer covered its operating costs opened two specialty centers within the building. Designed specifically to increase revenue, the Women's Center and the Seventh Floor cater to high-income patients who are willing to pay larger fees for premium service. "Profit" from these centers subsidizes other hospital services.

Challenge #2: The Increasing Demand for Services

Unfortunately, cutbacks in government funding have come just when the need for service is increasing. AIDS, illiteracy, homelessness, substance abuse, child abuse, poverty, and numerous other problems are at an all-time high and are expected to increase. As a result, nonprofits are seeing more clients, often in more dire condition, with fewer funds to meet their needs. If there was ever a time to do more with less, this is it.

The entrepreneurial nonprofit response: Entrepreneurial nonprofits have turned to volunteers to stretch their resources. They have learned to train volunteers effectively and efficiently, and they have learned how to keep volunteers motivated in order to keep them coming back. For example:

- Organizations that support people with AIDS have developed in most urban areas. These agencies rely on vast cadres of volunteers to cook, clean, bathe, shop for, and visit people with AIDS. The work is not easy: volunteers must perform the chores they most hate doing for themselves, and they must commit their time and their emotions to people who are dying. Despite the difficulties, AIDS volunteers are staunchly committed. Why? Because the nonprofit agencies have developed screening, training, management, and motivation techniques that make them *want* to work. They have, in effect, developed high-quality, nonpaid work forces on whom they can depend to carry out their mission.

Challenge #3: The Replacement of Grants with Government Contracts

As governments consolidate budgets, they are replacing grants to nonprofit agencies with fee-for-service contracts. This saves money for the government, but presents a problem for nonprofits. Grants provide funds for general operating overhead; fee-for-service contracts don't. As a result, nonprofits have lost much of the unrestricted money that kept the rent paid, the lights on, and their other programs operating. Some agencies have had to eliminate programs for which they don't get fee-for-service contracts.

The entrepreneurial nonprofit response: Entrepreneurial nonprofits are developing business ventures that can help pay for overhead and subsidize other programs. For example:

• A private, nonprofit senior center received funding from its county government to provide activity and outreach services for county seniors. When the grant was renewed, it was converted to a fee-for-service contract for a smaller range of services than the center was currently providing. The cuts included the salary of an outreach worker whose services would not be needed under the new contract. However, the center believed the outreach worker was an important part of its program. To fund her salary, it developed a small business called Grandma Services, which offered licensed short-term babysitting at the senior center and sold handmade items, such as sweaters and hats, made by clients of the center. Income from the business just covered the worker's salary.

Challenge #4: The Slowdown in Corporate Giving

Business is another big benefactor of nonprofit organizations. Given the economy, it's not surprising that corporate contributions have fallen off.

- The slower economy means there is less to give.
- The spate of mergers and acquisitions has reduced the number of givers.
- Those companies that survived restructuring are saddled with debt.
- The 1986 Tax Reform Act lowered the top corporate tax rate, effectively increasing the cost of giving pretax dollars.
- Several large corporations with long traditions of corporate giving have been bought by foreign owners who don't share that tradition.
- Many companies are offering corporate volunteers and in-kind contributions in lieu of cash.

As a result, many nonprofits have had to scale back programs, trim staffs, forgo pay raises, and further tighten their operations.

The entrepreneurial nonprofit response: Entrepreneurial nonprofits have begun to decrease their dependence on fund-raising and develop new ways to *earn* money. Strategies range from the sale of products and services related to the agencies' missions to the development of freestanding, for-profit businesses whose revenues subsidize the organization. For example:

- Numerous museums have developed lines of products featuring items in their collections. Some have licensed these products to outside manufacturers; others produce and sell the products themselves.

- A public radio station earns money by producing and selling customized music tracks for parties and other events for its city's subway system.
- A nonprofit hospital uses its kitchen to run a for-profit catering business.

Challenge #5: The Trend Toward Accountability

As money gets tighter, businesses are holding nonprofits increasingly accountable for the money they receive. They are evaluating nonprofits' fiscal health and management before making grants to make sure their investments will be well spent. They are favoring one-time-only grants, encouraging nonprofit recipients to become self-sufficient. They are offering matching grants, requiring nonprofits to augment their dollars with funds from other sources. And they are evaluating funded programs for effectiveness. This trend has added to the fundraising pressures already felt by nonprofits. While the demands are reasonable, they mean more hoops to jump through to raise the necessary cash.

The entrepreneurial nonprofit response: Entrepreneurial nonprofits have responded to the new requirements by becoming more businesslike in their operations. They have strengthened their money management systems. They have developed long-term funding strategies that blend fund-raising with earned income. They have developed cost-benefit evaluation systems for assessing their programs' effectiveness. And they have become more sophisticated in cultivating new funders and business partners, looking at potential partners' needs as well as their own. For example:

- A corporation that had long supported a local museum with major annual donations was forced, because of business slowdowns, to cancel future pledges. In response, the museum was compelled to develop its first serious long-range business plan, devising a variety of income streams to replace and augment the lost donation. These included increasing admission fees; renting museum spaces for private parties; expanding the museum gift shop; offering fee-based special events; expanding use of the museum restaurant to capture evening traffic; and cultivating new donors. When finished, the plan projected budgets with small surpluses for each of the following three years.

Challenge #6: The Rise of Strategic Philanthropy

The rise of strategic philanthropy, as discussed in Chapter 5, has caused considerable hand-wringing among nonprofits. Many fear the bottom-line approach will jeopardize their ability to raise money.

The entrepreneurial nonprofit response: While others debate its merits, entrepreneurial nonprofits have adopted a marketing approach. Recognizing the commercial value of their names and logos, they now ask companies for a marketing partnership, rather than a donation to a worthy cause. For example:

• A regional animal shelter with branches in several cities was seeking general operating funds, so it asked itself the logical question: what corporation would benefit from an association with our name and cause? Several logical partners came to mind: a pet food manufacturer, a pet store chain, a maker of pet products. The shelter approached a pet store chain whose stores overlapped the shelter's region. Together they developed a public education campaign that emphasized the importance of spaying and neutering. The campaign also built business for both partners. It advertised that if people bought pets from the store during a specified period, the shelter would spay or neuter their pets for half the regular price. (The chain's foundation paid the other half.) During the same period, people who came to the shelter to get a pet would get discount coupons to use at the pet store

chain. The chain used foundation money to fund the educational program and used money from marketing budgets for the coupon program
and ads. As a result of the program, the shelter furthered its mission,
and the pet store strengthened its image and its business.

Challenge #7: Increased Competition for Individual Donors

Individual contributions to nonprofits are growing. Unfortunately,
so is the number of nonprofits. As a result, competition for individual
donors is at an all-time high. For many nonprofits, this means a need
to buckle down and do more of the same: buy more mailing lists, send
more form letters, make more cold calls . . . and cross your fingers
that enough people will respond.

The entrepreneurial nonprofit response: Entrepreneurial
nonprofits are trying something new—marketing. They are wooing
new donors the same way business woos clients: by targeting selected
groups and developing strategies aimed specifically at them. Among
other things, they are developing marketing partnerships with corporations to win the attention of their customers; doing market research
to locate their best donors and learn how to appeal to them effectively;
and developing special events designed to attract potential donors.

Challenge #8: Increasing Expenses

For nonprofits as for business, money is shrinking and expenses
are expanding. (The biggest and fastest-growing expense is employee
health care.) Since most nonprofits don't offer products or services
with built-in profit, increasing fees won't solve the problem. They can

cut costs, but since nonprofit shops are already lean, cutting costs generally means cutting programs.

The entrepreneurial nonprofit response: Entrepreneurial nonprofits have responded to the challenge by developing revenue-producing ventures with built-in profits. The profits help pay for overhead and add a cushion against inflation. For example:

- A crime prevention organization wanted to develop a revenue-producing product that it could also use to further its message. After weighing several ideas, the organization decided to produce a "home safety kit," containing "burglar buster" window stickers, a safety audit checklist, a phone tag with emergency numbers, and other safety items. To avoid upfront costs, the organization presold the kit to a home security company. The company put its logo on the cover and paid for the printing of 200,000 kits. The nonprofit now sells the kits in bulk to other organizations. Police departments, PTA's, Junior Leagues, and other civic organizations buy the kits to distribute to their members. The crime prevention organization is getting its message out *and* making 100 percent profit, risk-free.

Challenge #9: Competition from Business

Business is slowly moving into the realm of social services. Child care, health care, education, substance abuse, elder care, recreation, and other areas that have traditionally been the domain of nonprofits are now becoming lucrative fields for business. In some areas corporations are contracting with government to provide services; in others they are developing businesses to meet the growing needs. As a result, nonprofits must now compete with business for both government contracts and clients. This puts additional strain on organizations already subject to numerous external pressures.

The entrepreneurial nonprofit response: Entrepreneurial nonprofits have risen to the challenge two ways. They have become more businesslike—strengthening management, redesigning pricing and financial systems, implementing marketing techniques—in order to meet the competition head-on. And they have developed business partnerships with for-profits in order to offer services jointly. For example:

- A nonprofit organization that teaches outdoor survival skills suddenly found itself facing competition from several corporations. Realizing that these for-profits had dollars and marketing power that outstripped theirs, the nonprofit decided to level the playing field. It hired a marketing director from the private sector, who helped it map out a long-term strategy for diversifying audience and income. With his help, the nonprofit divided the market into several categories: corporate clients, school districts, upscale urbanites, teenagers, women, and inner-city youths on scholarships. It then developed service and income goals for each group and low-budget, but targeted, marketing campaigns for each. As a result of the plan, income and attendance have significantly increased.
- A nonprofit organization teaches businesses about the hazards of tobacco smoke in the workplace and helps companies develop smoking policies. Recently several large national consulting firms have begun offering similar services. With nationally recognized names, large staffs, and big marketing budgets, these consultants presented formidable competition. So the nonprofit approached one with an offer: *We are a recognized expert in the smoking field, with ten years of experience and the endorsement of the U.S. surgeon general behind us. You have to learn this issue from scratch and face our competition in the process. Instead of competing, why not be partners? Your size and marketing strength combined with our expertise and credibility will make us unbeatable.* The for-profit agreed. It now hires the nonprofit on a contract basis to do its consulting on smoking policy.

Help from the Private Sector

Given the tenor of the times, many nonprofits would have found these entrepreneurial behaviors on their own. But as it happens, they've had help. Renegades from the private sector—people who lost their jobs to restructurings or wanted more meaningful work than business offered—have traded over to the nonprofit side. These new executives run their agencies the way they used to run their businesses—with the expectation that they will show a surplus at the end of the year. The only difference is that here, instead of paying the surplus out to stockholders, they plow it back into programs to help the agencies better meet their missions.

To help them run their shops, they are hiring M.B.A.'s and installing them as marketing directors and financial officers. They are sending veteran staffers to business seminars at Harvard and the Wharton School. They are bringing business consultants in to help them tackle specific problems.

There are clashes, to be sure. The nonprofit culture is still quite different from the corporate world. Decisions require consensus. More people—volunteers, staff, board members—must be involved. All decisions must be weighed against the mission, regardless of economic benefit.

But within the mission-driven structure things are changing. The old "nonprofit virginity" is gone, replaced with a lust for enterprise. Blatant distrust of business has been replaced with the knowledge that business strategies can meet nonprofit goals. Gradually, these new nonprofits are carving a territory in which the merger of mission and market form a powerful team.

CHAPTER 28

How to Work with a Nonprofit Partner

After reviewing the financial statements for the preceding quarter, the CEO called the comptroller and the VP for marketing into his office. "We're in trouble," he said. "We need to do a better job." After a short discussion, the two executives returned to their departments. "Just talked to the boss," said the comptroller to the staff. "We need to increase profits. Better look at boosting prices." Meanwhile, back in the marketing department, the VP gathered the troops. "Boss says we're in trouble," the VP told them. "Need to increase sales. Guess we better look at a price cut."

Ever notice how many problems occur simply because people are talking *at* each other instead of *to* each other? Having practiced now for several thousand years, you'd think we'd be better able to communicate. But of course, as anyone who's ever been a parent, or a spouse, or a teacher, or a businessperson, can tell you, the majority of problems in any relationship occur because of poor communication.

Public purpose partnerships are no different. When problems crop up between the partners—which they do—it's almost always because people aren't talking clearly—or listening attentively. For example: one partner expects the other to do something by a certain time. The partner with the obligation is running late. But instead of warning the other party that there's going to be a problem, on the appointed day the partner just doesn't deliver. Who wouldn't get upset?

Here's another example: the partners agree that their special event will be jointly staffed by company employees and nonprofit volunteers. However, they fail to specify how many staffers each side will provide. On the day of the event, thirty volunteers show up, but only five employees. The volunteers are swamped; the nonprofit team is furious. Who's at fault? If they had specified numbers ahead of time, each side could have recruited the needed number and the problem would have been avoided.

Here's one more: in the joy of partnership, the partners fail to consider how their program will be presented to the press. During an interview, the nonprofit's public relations person neglects to name each of the corporate divisions that are participating in the program. The division managers are angry. Of course, the problem wouldn't have occurred had they talked the issue through ahead of time.

All these problems occurred because of poor communication. The partners had different expectations of what would happen. Reality disappointed them, and tensions arose.

These are not merely hypothetical cases. These are the types of problems most likely to waylay a partnership campaign. It is precisely these kinds of procedural factors that bog a partnership down. Fortunately there's a relatively easy cure.

- Think through every aspect of your campaign before it begins.
- Define roles and responsibilities clearly at the outset.
- Build in communication checkpoints to make sure both partners' needs are being met.

If you do those things you can avoid surprises. And in partnerships, as in financial statements, no surprise is a good surprise.

Managing the Relationship

There are a few other things you can do to keep your relationship running smoothly. Most partnerships have problems in the same places—the places where corporate and nonprofit cultures clash. Anticipating those frictions—and planning ahead—can minimize tensions. Here are some specific recommendations for keeping the relationship running well.

Timelines

The majority of partnership problems concern timelines. Campaigns tend to be driven by marketplace needs and often require fast decisions, which, unfortunately, are not a nonprofit's strength. But there are things both sides can do to minimize problems.

You can anticipate the culture of the nonprofit, including those factors that tend to slow down decision-making: reliance on volunteers, part-time staff, the need for consensus. Anticipating the problem won't make it go away, but may make it easier to deal with.

The nonprofit can keep the number of people involved in decisions to a minimum by appointing a committee (rather than the whole board) to decide on policy issues, and by using a small committee of key players to make campaign operating decisions. The nonprofit can also assign people with a marketing or business background to work on the campaign.

Additionally, as you work together to plan your campaign, try to do the following:

- Create realistic (rather than optimistic) time frames for the project.
- Give the schedule more breathing room than you might if you were working alone.
- Make sure that all delivery, review, and sign-off dates are clearly spelled out ahead of time.

Spelling Out Roles and Responsibilities

Spelling out both parties' roles and responsibilities at the outset will prevent misunderstandings later. It will enable you to develop the program so that both sides get what they want. It will also help you understand how the other side thinks. To do it, you'll need to walk through every aspect of the campaign, considering everything that might happen—desirable and undesirable, expected and unexpected.

Here are some things to think through and spell out in writing:

• **Goals:** What does each partner want to get out of the campaign? Be as specific as possible in terms of exposure, money, press, sales gains, etc. Are your goals compatible? or do they point up potential areas of conflict? Now is the time to resolve them.

• **Permissions, reviews, vetoes:** Spell out who can review what and when, and who can veto what and when. When can you use the nonprofit's name and logo? When can't you? When can the nonprofit use yours? Are all elements of the program to be jointly reviewed? Is all campaign material to be jointly reviewed?

• **Exclusivity:** Is this relationship exclusive? If so, for how long? When will it end? If not, what other types of corporations or nonprofits can become involved with one or both partners? Can either partner review and veto a new prospective partner?

• **Promotion:** How will the campaign be promoted? in what media? to what target audiences? Are certain types of promotion off-limits? Who decides?

• **Money:** How will money be raised? How much money do you expect the campaign to make? How will it be managed? How will it be distributed, and when? Will minimum and maximum amounts go to the nonprofit? Are there guarantees? What auditing procedures will be used?

• **Ownership:** Who will own the campaign material? the ideas? the copyrights? If you plan a continuing relationship, do you need a licensing agreement?

• **Reporting:** What reports will you generate at the end: money raised? sales figures? market research results? Who will see the reports? Who will pay for them? How will you report the results to the public?

- **Termination:** When do you want the relationship to end? What might make it end sooner? later? How will you deal with those eventualities?

- **Roles and responsibilities:** Who will do what in each organization? Will you use the nonprofit's staff? its local chapters? its volunteers? How many? For what tasks? What role will your employees play? your sales force? your franchisees? your retailers? Who will coordinate the campaign elements? How much time will this take? What if you need to hire additional people: who will pay?

Obviously this list is not exhaustive, nor can you know every answer before the campaign begins. But thinking through and discussing these questions will help both partners clarify and articulate their expectations. They will point up areas of potential conflict so that they can be resolved before the campaign begins rather than during its implementation.

Using Consultants

Some companies that develop public purpose campaigns use consultants to do so. Most often this happens when a consultant brings an idea for a campaign to a corporation and the corporation decides to participate. The consultants are generally special-events planners, marketing firms, or public relations firms.

Are consultants a good idea? It depends on your organization. A clear advantage of using a consultant is prior experience. If the consultant has managed partnerships in the past, he or she can remove some of the headaches for you. The consultant can help you find an appropriate partner, and then play buffer between you. He or she can develop and critique ideas with relative objectivity, and can manage the details of the event, sparing both your staff and that of the nonprofit.

How much are those benefits worth? The answer, again, depends on the corporation. They are probably worth more to a company trying a partnership for the first time than to one that's experienced. Experienced organizations are often better off on their own, since they'll have learned how to work with a nonprofit and how to tailor a campaign to their own needs.

CHAPTER 29

Nonprofits and Legal Issues

I don't know as I want a lawyer to tell me what I cannot do. I hire him to tell me how to do what I want to do.

—J. P. Morgan

Morgan knew that you can see regulations in one of two ways, as restricting or as enabling, and he chose the latter. It's much the more useful attitude—in partnerships as in any other kind of business. In fact, the regulations governing partnerships are neither complicated nor restrictive. Nothing in the legal regulations or tax codes should stand in your way. This chapter discusses the most basic regulations governing public purpose partnerships. For more detailed and up-to-date information, consult a lawyer and a tax accountant before proceeding.

Legal Issues in Partnership Campaigns

Ventures that raise money for nonprofits are regulated by the states, with requirements varying from state to state. The regulations are not troublesome—they concern primarily the filing of documents and some contract language—but following them is essential. So before undertaking a campaign, learn the regulations in every state in which the campaign will operate.

State regulations call partnership campaigns "commercial co-venturer agreements." Corporations that partner nonprofits are called "commercial co-venturers." Ventures that raise money for nonprofits by tying a donation directly to the purchase or use of a company's product or service are called "charitable sales promotions."

Only two states—Maine and Massachusetts—require corporations to file with the state as "professional solicitors" because they are raising money for nonprofits. A few other states require that the contract between the nonprofit and the corporation be filed with the state. The majority of states require only that the partners have a contract and that it stipulate the terms of the agreement and the way information will be disclosed to the public.

One thing to be aware of is that in some states the way the money is given to the nonprofit makes a difference. If the company contributes an amount per product or service purchased, there's no problem. However, if the company offers to pass on donations made by the public, the company may be considered a "solicitor," that is, a fundraiser for the organization. Being a solicitor is not necessarily a problem; but it may mean additional regulatory hoops to jump through, and possibly additional expenses.

Once you've sketched out your campaign, check with the attorney general of each state in which it will operate. Or talk with a law firm that is familiar with nonprofit fund-raising issues. The lawyers will be able to guide you through the regulations. You should also find out whether both you and the nonprofit are protected from fraud and whether additional insurance is required.

Corporate Donors and the IRS

Corporate donations to nonprofits are tax-deductible, up to a limit of 10 percent of the company's taxable income. That's the good news. The bad news is that companies are supposed to subtract from the donation the value of any benefit they get from the gift. For example, if you donate $1,000 to an orchestra and in exchange receive a free season pass worth $300, you are supposed to deduct from your taxable income only $700. The reality is that most companies take the full deduction and the IRS doesn't pay attention.

However, the IRS seems to be stepping up scrutiny in this area. As you'll read below, the agency is beginning to look more closely at corporate sponsorship fees paid to nonprofits. It may also decide to pay more attention to the dollar amount of deductions claimed.

There's no cause for alarm, however, because the portion of your gift that is not deductible as a charitable gift can be deducted as a business expense—as if you had bought that season pass for your business use. Either way, the end result is the same for you. What is more important in IRS scrutiny of partnerships is the effect on non-profit taxes.

Nonprofits and the IRS

Almost all nonprofit organizations are exempt from federal income tax. The government has granted them this exemption because they exist to serve a charitable (usually educational) mission rather than to make money, and the government is aiding them in this mission by excluding them from tax responsibility. But the government has also put caveats on the exemption to prevent nonprofits from operating businesses which would compete unfairly with for-profit companies. The caveats specify three criteria a nonprofit activity must meet in order to be taxable:

- it must be "unrelated to the organization's tax-exempt mission";
- it must be "regularly carried on"; and
- it must be deemed a "trade or business."

If an activity meets all three of these criteria its income will be subject to UBIT—Unrelated Business Income Tax. Few nonprofit activities meet all three.

The "substantially related" test is by far the most important. To be substantially related to an organization's mission, a venture must contribute in an "important way" to furthering that mission. It must not exist solely to make money. According to that definition, the operation of an off-campus fast-food franchise by a university is not related, but the sale of textbooks is, because textbooks further the university's mission of educating students. Income from a catering business run by a history museum is not related, but income from authentic Victorian dinners hosted by museum staff wearing period costumes is related, because such dinners further the museum's purpose of educating people about history.

To be "regularly carried on" an activity must be continuing, not occasional. If it is comparable to commercial activity, such as the running of a store, it is likely to be considered "regularly carried on." A one-time special event is not. Many nonprofits generate tax-free income from activities such as thrift stores, gift shops, and restaurants, which are regularly carried on. They are able to do so because of several exceptions to this regulation:

- the merchandise being sold is substantially related to the organization's mission; or
- the activity is conducted primarily by volunteers; or
- the bulk of the merchandise has been donated; or
- the activity is carried on primarily for the convenience of the organization's members, students, patients, volunteers, etc.; or
- the activity produces "passive income" such as rents, royalties, or dividends.

An activity that meets any one of these exceptions qualifies for tax exemption. Obviously, many nonprofit activities qualify.

Tightening the Exemption?

Primarily because of challenges by small-business owners, Congress and the IRS have considered changing the nonprofit tax code to make it tougher to qualify for tax exemption. They have focused primarily on the "substantially related" test, with threats to tighten the definition of relatedness. However, despite years of examination, very little has actually changed.

Short of actual changes in the code, though, the IRS has begun to look more critically at the tax returns of individual nonprofits, and has challenged the "relatedness" of certain income streams. Most notable of these, because they apply to corporate partnerships, are two cases in which the IRS ruled that sponsorship fees paid by corporations to organizers of college football bowl games were actually advertising fees, in exchange for which the corporations were given substantial advertising benefits. As advertising fees, the sponsorship fees are unrelated to the organizers' educational missions and are therefore taxable. In early 1992, as this book goes to press, both organizations have appealed the ruling, claiming that the sponsorship fees are not advertising, but merely corporate support of the games. They claim that placing the companies' names on the bowls and in the stadiums was an appropriate way of thanking the corporations for their gifts. However, it seems unlikely that the IRS will back down; in fact, most people believe the agency will cast the net wider, challenging other sponsorship fees as well.

What does this mean for corporate sponsorships? Nothing worrisome. First, these rulings apply only to event sponsorship, not to other forms of partnership. Second, a bill is pending in Congress which would exempt sponsorship fees paid to nonprofits from income tax. Third, there are many ways to structure an event sponsorship so that taxes will not be an issue:

1. Make sure your event is related to the nonprofit's mission. If your contribution is helping the nonprofit spread its message, there is little likelihood it will be challenged by the IRS.

2. Reduce the appearance of advertising benefits. If you sponsor an event, don't name the event after your corporation. Say it is "sponsored by" or "brought to you by" your company, rather than calling it the X Corporation Event.

3. Balance the benefits to the company with benefits to the public. Make sure the public receives as much benefit from the event as you do.

4. Avoid itemizing benefits to the company in written contracts. Keep that part of your agreement verbal. If the IRS were to see an itemized list of benefits it would have solid grounds to consider your sponsorship advertising.

5. Consider structuring your sponsorship as a licensing agreement because royalty payments to nonprofits are tax-exempt. For instance, if you sponsor a cleanup of a park with a local environmental group, instead of putting your logo on volunteers' T-shirts (which could be construed as advertising), license the nonprofit's logo to put on T-shirts you produce and give out. That way you will be paying for the advertising, and your payment to the nonprofit will be in the form of tax-exempt royalties.

6. Don't brag. It's to be hoped that your event sponsorship will attract a lot of press. But don't brag about the amount generated. That could cause the IRS to get suspicious, thinking *you* think of the event as advertising.

7. Stay small. The IRS is not interested in cracking down on every partnership event. It has gone after the big, visible guys, hoping to encourage voluntary compliance with its regulations. The agency won't be looking at every—or even most—events in the future. You can sponsor nonprofit events with no cause for concern.

In any event, you should understand that *your* taxes are not affected by these regulations. Only nonprofits are being taxed. The only impact on corporations will come if nonprofits, knowing they will be stung, increase their sponsorship fees to cover the tax bite. But even this is unlikely except in a very few cases, since the majority of nonprofits will find ways to avoid the tax.

What About Other Forms of Partnership?

Nonprofit tax liability has virtually no impact on other forms of partnership as we've discussed them here. The types of ventures described in this book should not be taxable. Cause-related marketing campaigns provide donations to nonprofits; donations are not taxable. Licensing agreements provide "passive" royalty payments to nonprofits; passive income is not taxable. If you purchase a premium item from a nonprofit, that item should be related to the organization's mission, educating your customers about the cause; related income is not taxable. If you purchase a continuing service from a nonprofit—say, classes for your employees taught by social service workers, or street maintenance outside your shop performed by job trainees—that service should be related to the organization's mission; its income, therefore, would not be taxable. And if you sponsor a special event with a nonprofit, the event should be designed to attract attention to or educate the public about the cause; again, related income is not taxable.

The bottom line for you in developing a partnership is to build your venture around the nonprofit's mission—and that shouldn't be a problem. After all, one of the reasons you're forming the partnership is to educate the public about your partner's cause. Stay true to that goal and you'll be in the clear.

That's not to say that your partner may not worry. Nonprofits fear taxes like the plague. Some will avoid partnerships just for fear of inviting IRS scrutiny. If your prospective partner is concerned, talk to a nonprofit tax attorney, who can help you design a program that is clearly tax-exempt. Fear of taxes should not stand in the way of your partnership.

Rules of Thumb for Working with a Nonprofit

1. Anticipate the nature of nonprofits:
   - All decisions will be weighed against the mission.
   - The nonprofit will have concerns about implied endorsements.
   - The nonprofit may be slow to make decisions because of the need for consensus and the reliance on volunteers.
2. Think through every aspect of your campaign before it begins.
3. Define roles and responsibilities clearly at the outset.
4. Create realistic (rather than optimistic) time frames.
5. Build in communication checkpoints to make sure both partners' needs are being met.
6. Make sure that all delivery, review, and sign-off dates are clearly spelled out ahead of time.
7. Be flexible.

Index